Favourite
ANIMAL
POEMS

Edited by SAMUEL CARR

Illustrated from wood engravings by
THOMAS BEWICK

CHANCELLOR
PRESS

"I think I could turn and live with animals,
they are so placid and self-contain'd . . ."
                                Walt Whitman

First published in Great Britain in 1990 by
Chancellor Press
Michelin House
81 Fulham Road
London SW3 6RB

Introduction © Samuel Carr 1990
Design and arrangement © Octopus Books Limited 1990

ISBN 1 85152 098 8

Typeset by MS Filmsetting Limited, Frome, Somerset
Printed in Czechoslovakia
50759

CONTENTS

INTRODUCTION

Most animal poems are concerned as much with their authors' feelings as with the character of their ostensible subjects. In the case of fable-writers like Aesop, La Fontaine and John Gay the animals are anthropomorphised into human beings so that few of their native qualities remain. Even when the animal, bird or fish is seen realistically, it is often the poet's reaction to his theme rather than the individual character of the creature in question which provides the poem's focus. John Clare, by contrast, was one of the few poets who could forget himself while concentrating on the particular animal, bird or fish about which he was writing. In this anthology the emphasis is on the animals themselves rather than on the poets through whose eyes they are seen.

Except in the case of sentimental nineteenth-century painters like Landseer, the same difficulty does not arise with the representations of the artists. While a woodcut by Bewick, a mezzotint by Stubbs, a Dürer Owl or a Géricault Horse are at once recognisable as the work of their creators, it is the creature in question rather than the ideas and feelings of the artist which takes the viewer's attention.

The woodcuts of Thomas Bewick (1753–1828) illustrate this book. Bewick was born at Cherryburn in Northumberland. After an unsuccessful attempt to establish himself professionally as a wood-engraver in London, he returned to the North of England. There he and a partner ran a flourishing – but financially not very rewarding – business as jobbing engravers at Newcastle upon Tyne. If an illustration for a lottery ticket, an auction sale, a bill head, a trade card or even a bank note was required, the firm could be relied upon to produce exactly what was wanted in the form of a wood block, ready for printing, with the appropriate lettering cut into it.

During a long working life Bewick produced several

thousand such designs. To-day, however, he is best remembered for the books which he himself wrote and illustrated: *A General History of Quadrupeds* (1790) and *A History of British Birds* (two volumes, 1797 and 1804). A similar project dealing with Fishes should have appeared, but only a few of the illustrations were cut before Bewick died. It is from these works that the majority of the illustrations in this book have been taken. While their scientific accuracy reflects Bewick's expert knowledge as a natural historian of the British countryside, sometimes, where more exotic creatures were concerned, the artist was obliged to substitute imagination for first-hand observation. His Oran-Outang (or Wild Man of the Woods), for instance, has an implausible air as he sits nonchalantly on a bench with a staff in his hand, and the pouch-less 'Kanguroo' makes an unconvincing marsupial.

To return from the pictures to the poetry, it was thought that light verse could not of its nature be serious. So far from this being true, even so-called nonsense poetry can contain personal depths of meaning and emotion. Edward Lear's poems, for instance, are so memorable, so funny and so touching because they mirror not only Lear's most personal feelings, but the human condition in general. So, no apology is needed for the inclusion here of some light verse, jokes and nonsense. The only cause for regret is that there have been few poets so gifted in this way as Lewis Carroll and Lear. One such, however, was John Hookham Frere. His *The Loves of the Triangles*, (an extract appears on page 235) shows that he had a gift for inspired nonsense which, alas, was left undeveloped. (Incidentally, the Frere poem is a satire on Erasmus Darwin's bathetic *The Loves of the Plants,* from which the fanciful account of the Whale on page 143 is taken.)

With certain animals such as the Horse, the Cat and the Dog there is a superfluity of poems to choose from and the difficulty was to decide which ones to include. Similarly, with certain birds like the Nightingale, the Owl, the Blackbird and the Thrush, on each of which many different poets have written, it has seemed best not to exclude particular poems because of their comparative familiarity, but to choose the appropriate one, whether well-known or obscure. The surprising thing is that there are so few poems on what, in the abstract, might seem poetically sympathetic creatures. There are rather few Fish poems, for example, and how many poets have celebrated the Lion? Indeed, it is only in the last two centuries that poets have written about individual animals. Lesbia's Sparrow, about which Catullus wrote one of the most famous of all animal poems, is an exception to this rule, and so too is *Poly-Olbion* by Michael Drayton, where many highly particularised creatures are so curiously catalogued. But it remains true that before William Cowper in the later 18th century, poets tended to write of animals in general, just as they wrote generalised pastoral descriptions of the landscapes in which the animals lived.

The final section of the book is concerned with Mythical Creatures, ranging from the Phoenix, the Dragon or the Kraken, to the Jabberwocky, the Pobble or the Quangle Wangle, but just because none of them ever existed was thought an insufficient reason for their exclusion. That Thomas Bewick was little interested in making woodcuts of them is, from our point of view, a pity. Even his Cameleopard appears under somewhat false pretences for, although you might not guess it from the picture, it was really supposed to be a Giraffe.

ACKNOWLEDGMENT

The Publishers gratefully acknowledge the following for permission to reproduce copyright poems:

For 'The Pike', by Edmund Blunden, to William Collins Sons & Co. Ltd.; for 'Shark', by Lord Alfred Douglas, to Edward Coleman Esq. and B. T. Batsford Ltd; for 'Chipmunk's Day', by Randall Jarrell, from *The Bat-Poet* (Kestrel Books, 1977) copyright © 1963, 1964 by Macmillan Publishing Co., Inc., New York, and Penguin Books Ltd., London; for 'Wasp in a Room', by Elizabeth Jennings, to the Author and David Higham Associates Ltd.; for 'The Centaurs', by Rudyard Kipling, to A. P. Watt Ltd. on behalf of the National Trust; for 'Kangaroo', by D. H. Lawrence, from *The Complete Poems of D. H. Lawrence*, edited and collected by Vivian de Sola Pinto and F. Warren Roberts. Copyright © 1964, 1971 by Angelo Ravagli and C. M. Weekley, Executors of the Estate of Frieda Lawrence. All rights reserved. Reprinted by permission of Viking Penguin, a division of Penguin Books USA, Inc.; 'The Corncrake', by Louis MacNeice, from *The Collected Poems of Louis MacNeice*, reprinted by permission of Faber and Faber Ltd.; 'Jellyfish', by Marianne Moore, from *The Complete Poems of Marianne Moore*. All rights reserved. Reprinted by permission of Viking Penguin Inc., New York, and Faber and Faber Ltd., London; 'Caged Lion' and 'The Bat', by Ruth Pitter, reproduced by permission of Parrot and Coales, Solicitors, and Century Hutchinson; for 'Hedgehog', by Anthony Thwaite (from *Poems, 1953–1983*), to the Author.

THE CREATION OF ANIMALS

from: The Book of Genesis

And God said, Let the waters bring forth abundantly the moving creature that hath life, and fowl that *may fly above the earth in the open firmament of heaven.*

And God created great whales, and every living creature that moveth, which the waters brought forth abundantly, after their kind, and every winged fowl after his kind: and God saw that it was *good.*

And God blessed them, saying, Be fruitful, and multiply, and fill the waters in the seas, and let fowl multiply in the earth.

And the evening and morning were the fifth day.

And God said, Let the earth bring forth the living creature after his kind, cattle, and creeping thing, and beast of the earth after his kind; and it was so.

And God made the beast of the earth after his kind, and cattle after their kind, and every thing that creepeth upon the earth after his kind; and God saw that it was *good.*

The
CREATION
of
BIRDS

THE CREATION OF BIRDS

from: Paradise Lost (Book VII)

And let the Fowle be multiply'd on the Earth.
Flying, and over Lands with mutual wing
Easing thir flight; so stears the prudent Crane
Her annual Voiage, born on Windes; the Aire
Floats, as they pass, fann'd with unnumber'd plumes:
From Branch to Branch the smaller Birds with song
Solac'd the Woods, and spred thir painted wings
Till Ev'n, nor then the solemn Nightingal
Ceas'd warbling, but all night tun'd her soft layes:
Others on Silver Lakes and Rivers Bath'd
Thir downie Brest; the Swan with Arched neck
Between her white wings mantling proudly, Rowes
Her state with Oarie feet: yet oft they quit
The Dank, and rising on stiff Pennons, towre
The mid Aereal Skie: Others on ground
Walk'd firm; the crested Cock whose clarion sounds
The silent hours, and th' other whose gay Traine
Adorns him, colour'd with the Florid hue
Of Rainbows and Starrie Eyes.

JOHN MILTON [1608–1674]

GOLDFINCHES

Sometimes goldfinches one by one will drop
From low-hung branches: little space they stop;
But sip, and twitter, and their feathers sleek;
Then off at once, as in a wanton freak:
Or perhaps, to show their black and golden wings,
Pausing upon their yellow flutterings.

JOHN KEATS [1795–1821]

THE COCK

from: The Nonnes Preestes Tale

A yeerd she hadde, enclosed al aboute
With stikkes, and a drye dych withoute,
In which she hadde a cok, hight Chauntecleer.
In al the land, of crowyng nas his peer.
His voys was murier than the murie orgon
On messe-dayes that in the chirche gon.
Wel sikerer was his crowying in his logge
Than is a clokke or an abbey orlogge.
By nature he knew ech ascencioun
Of the equynoxial in thilke toun;
For whan degrees fiftene weren ascended,
Thanne crew he, that it myghte nat been amended.
His coomb was redder than the fyn coral,
And batailled as it were a castel wal;
His byle was blak, and as the jeet it shoon;
Lyk asure were his legges and his toon;
His nayles whitter than the lylye flour,
And lyk the burned gold was his colour.
This gentil cok hadde in his governaunce
Sevene hennes for to doon al his plesaunce,
Whiche were his sustres and his paramours,
And wonder lyk to hym, as of colours;
Of whiche the fairest hewed on hir throte
Was cleped faire damoysel Pertelote.

GEOFFREY CHAUCER [1343–1400]

19

THE ROBIN

Poore bird! I doe not envie thee;
Pleas'd in the gentle Melodie
    Of thy owne Song.
Let crabbed winter Silence all
The winged Quire; he never shall
    Chaine up thy Tongue:
        Poor Innocent!
When I would please my selfe, I looke on thee;
And guess some sparkes of the Felicitie,
    That Selfe-Content.

When the bleake Face of winter Spreads
The Earth, and violates the Meads
    Of all their Pride;
When Sapless Trees and Flowers are fled,
Back to their Causes, and lye dead
    To all beside:
        I see thee Set,
Bidding defiance to the bitter Ayre,
Upon a wither'd Spray; by cold made bare,
    And drooping yet.

There, full in notes, to ravish all
My Earth, I wonder what to call
    My dullness; when
I heare thee, prettie Creature, bring
Thy better odes of Praise, and Sing,
    To puzzle men:
        Poore pious Elfe!
I am instructed by thy harmonie,
To sing the Time's uncertaintie,
    Safe in my Selfe.

Poore Redbreast, caroll out thy Laye,
And teach us mortalls what to saye.
    Here cease the Quire
Of ayerie Choristers; noe more
Mingle your notes; but catch a Store
From her Sweet Lire;
    You are but weake,
Mere summer Chanters; you have neither wing
Nor voice, in winter. Prettie Redbreast, Sing,
    What I would speake.

GEORGE DANIEL [1616–1657]

IN PRAISE OF BIRDS

from: Jubilate Agno

Let Asaph rejoice with the Nightingale – The
musician of the Lord! and the watchman of the
Lord!

Let Shema rejoice with the Glowworm, who is the
lamp of the traveller and mead of the musician.

Let Jeduthun rejoice with the Woodlark, who is
sweet and various.

Let Chenaniah rejoice with Chloris, in the vivacity of
his powers and the beauty of his person.

Let Gideoni rejoice with the Goldfinch, who is shrill
and loud, and full withal.

Let Giddalti rejoice with the Mocking-bird, who
takes off the notes of the Aviary and reserves his
own.

Let Jogli rejoice with the Linnet, who is distinct and
of mild delight.

Let Benjamin bless and rejoice with the Redbird, who
is soft and soothing.

Let Dan rejoice with the Blackbird, who praises God
with all his heart, and biddeth to be of good cheer.

Let Elizur rejoice with the Partridge, who is a
prisoner of state and is proud of his keepers.

Let Shedeur rejoice with Pyrausta, who dwelleth in
a medium of fire, which God hath adapted for
him.

Let Shelumiel rejoice with Olor, who is of a goodly
savour, and the very look of him harmonizes the
mind.

Let Jael rejoice with the Plover, who whistles for his
live, and foils the marksmen and their guns.

Let Raguel rejoice with the Cock of Portugal – God
send good Angels to the allies of England!

Let Hobab rejoice with Necydalus, who is the Greek
of a Grub.

Let Zurishaddai with the Polish Cock rejoice – The
Lord restore peace to Europe.

Let Zuar rejoice with the Guinea Hen – The Lord add
to his mercies in the WEST!
Let Chesed rejoice with Strepsiceros, whose weapons
are the ornaments of his peace.
Let Hagar rejoice with Gnesion, who is the right sort
of eagle, and towers the highest.
Let Libni rejoice with the Redshank, who migrates
not but is translated to the upper regions.
Let Nahshon rejoice with the Seabreese, the Lord
give the sailors of his Spirit.
Let Helon rejoice with the Woodpecker – the Lord
encourage the propagation of trees!
Let Amos rejoice with the Coote——prepare to meet
thy God, O Israel.

CHRISTOPHER SMART [1722–1771]

THE DALLIANCE OF THE EAGLES

Skirting the river road, (my forenoon walk, my rest,)
Skyward in air a sudden muffled sound, the dalliance of the
    eagles,
The rushing amorous contact high in space together,
The clinching interlocking claws, a living, fierce, gyrating wheel,
Four beating wings, two beaks, a swirling mass tight grappling
In tumbling turning clustering loops, straight downward
    falling,
Till o'er the river pois'd, the twain yet one, a moment's lull,
A motionless still balance in the air, then parting, talons
    loosing,
Upward again on slow-firm pinions slanting, their separate
    diverse flight,
She hers, he his, pursuing.

WALT WHITMAN [1819–1892]

24

A WREN'S NEST

Among the dwellings framed by birds
   In field or forest with nice care,
Is none that with the little Wren's
   In snugness may compare.

No door the tenement requires,
   And seldom needs a laboured roof;
Yet is it to the fiercest sun
   Impervious, and storm-proof.

So warm, so beautiful withal,
   In perfect fitness for its aim,
That to the Kind by special grace
   Their instinct surely came.

And when for their abodes they seek
　　An opportune recess,
The hermit has no finer eye
　　For shadowy quietness.

These find, 'mid ivied abbey-walls,
　　A canopy in some still nook;
Others are pent-housed by a brae
　　That overhangs a brook.

There to the brooding bird her mate
　　Warbles by fits his low clear song;
And by the busy streamlet both
　　Are sung to all day long.

Or in sequestered lanes they build,
　　Where, till the flitting bird's return,
Her eggs within the nest repose,
　　Like relics in an urn.

But still, where general choice is good,
　　There is a better and a best;
And, among fairest objects, some
　　Are fairer than the rest;

This, one of those small builders proved
　　In a green covert, where, from out
The forehead of a pollard oak,
　　The leafy antlers sprout;

For She who planned the mossy lodge,
　　Mistrusting her evasive skill,
Had to a Primrose looked for aid
　　Her wishes to fulfil.

High on the trunk's projecting brow,
　And fixed an infant's span above
The budding flowers, peeped forth the nest
　The prettiest of the grove!

The treasure proudly did I show
　To some whose minds without disdain
Can turn to little things; but once
　Looked up for it in vain:

'Tis gone – a ruthless spoiler's prey,
　Who heeds not beauty, love, or song,
'Tis gone! (so seemed it) and we grieved
　Indignant at the wrong.

Just three days after, passing by
　In clearer light the moss-built cell
I saw, espied its shaded mouth;
　And felt that all was well.

The Primrose for a veil had spread
　The largest of her upright leaves;
And thus, for purposes benign,
　A simple flower deceives.

Concealed from friends who might disturb
　Thy quiet with no ill intent,
Secure from evil eyes and hands
　On barbarous plunder bent,

Rest, Mother-bird! and when thy young
　Take flight, and thou art free to roam,
When withered is the guardian Flower,
　And empty thy late home,

Think how ye prospered, thou and thine,
  Amid the unviolated grove,
Housed near the growing Primrose-tuft
  In foresight, or in love.

WILLIAM WORDSWORTH [1770–1850]

A SPARROW

from: Phylyp Sparowe

It was so prety a fole,
It wold syt on a stole,
And lerned after my scole
For to kepe his cut,
With, Phyllyp, kepe your cut!
   It had a veluet cap,
And wold syt vpon my lap,
And seke after small wormes,
And somtyme white bred crommes;
And many tymes and ofte
Betwene my brestes softe
It wolde lye and rest;
It was propre and prest.
   Sometyme he wolde gaspe
Whan he sawe a waspe;
A fly or a gnat,
He wolde flye at that;
And prytely he wold pant
Whan he saw an ant;
Lord, how he wolde pry
After the butterfly!
Lorde, how he wolde hop
After the gressop!
And whan I sayd, Phyp, Phyp,

Than he wold lepe and skyp,
And take me by the lyp.
Alas, it wyll me slo,
That Phillyp is gone me fro!
   Si in i qui ta tes,
Alas, I was euyll at ease!
De pro fun dis cla ma vi,
Whan I sawe my sparrowe dye!
   For it wold come and go,
And fly so to and fro;
And on me it wolde lepe
Whan I was aslepe,
And his fethers shake
Wherewith he wolde make
Me often for to wake,
And for to take him in
Vpon my naked skyn;
God wot, we thought no syn:
What though he crept so lowe?
It was no hurt, I trowe,
He dyd nothynge, perde,
But syt vpon my kne:
Phyllyp, though he were nyse,
In him it was no vyse;

Phyllyp had leue to go
To pyke my lytell too;
Phillip myght be bolde
And do what he wolde;
Phillip wolde seke and take
All the flees blake
That he coulde there espye
With his wanton eye.

JOHN SKELTON [1460–1529]

THE DEAD CANARY

from: Poor Matthias

Poor Matthias! – Found him lying
Fall'n beneath his perch and dying?
Found him stiff, you say, though warm –
All convulsed his little form?
Poor canary! many a year
Well he knew his mistress dear,
Now in vain you call his name,
Vainly raise his rigid frame,
Vainly warm him in your breast,
Vainly kiss his golden crest,
Smooth his ruffled plumage fine,
Touch his trembling beak with wine.
One more gasp – it is the end!
Dead and mute our tiny friend!
– Songster thou of many a year,
Now thy mistress brings thee here,
Says, it fits that I rehearse,
Tribute due to thee, a verse,
Meed for daily song of yore
Silent now for evermore.

MATTHEW ARNOLD [1822–1888]

ON A PEACOCK

Thou foolish Bird, of Feathers proud,
Whose Lustre yet thine Eyes ne're see:
The gazing Wonder of the Crowd,
Beauteous, not to thy self, but Me!
Thy Hellish Voice doth those affright,
Whose Eyes were charmed at thy sight.

Vainly thou think'st, those Eyes of thine
Were such as sleepy *Argus* lost;
When he was touch'd with rod Divine,
Who lat of Vigilance did boast.
Little at best they'll thee avail,
Not in thine *Head*, but in thy *Tayl*.

Wisemen do *forward* look to try
What will in *following* Moments come:
Backward thy useless Eyes do ly,
Nor do enquire of *future* doom.
'Nothing can remedy what's past;
Wisdom must guard the present cast.'

Our Eyes are best employ'd at home,
Not when they are on others plac'd:
From thine but little good can come,
Which never on thy self are cast:
What can of such a Tool be made:
A Tayl *well-furnish'd*, but an empty Head.

THOMAS HEYRICK [1649–1694]

THE YELLOWHAMMER

When shall I see the white-thorn leaves agen,
  And yellowhammers gathering the dry bents
By the dyke side, on stilly moor or fen,
  Feathered with love and nature's good intents?
Rude is the tent this architect invents,
  Rural the place, with cart ruts by dyke side.
Dead grass, horse hair, and downy-headed bents
  Tied to dead thistles – she doth well provide,
Close to a hill of ants where cowslips bloom
And shed oer meadows far their sweet perfume.
  In early spring, when winds blow chilly cold,
The yellowhammer, trailing grass, will come
To fix a place and choose an early home,
  With yellow breast and head of solid gold.

JOHN CLARE [1793–1864]

THE OSTRICH

from: Phylyp Sparowe

The ostrich, that will eat
An horseshoe so great,
In the stead of meat,
Such fervent heat
His stomach doth freat;
He cannot well fly,
Nor sing tunably,
Yet at a brayd
He hath well assayed
To sol-fa above ela.
Fa, lorell, fa, fa!
Ne quando
Male cantando,
The best that we can,
To make him our bell-man,
And let him ring the bells.
He can do nothing else.

JOHN SKELTON [1460–1529]

THE PARROT

The deep affections of the breast
  That Heaven to living things imparts
Are not exclusively possess'd
  By human hearts.

A parrot from the Spanish Main,
  Full young and early caged, came o'er
With bright wings to the bleak domain
  Of Mulla's shore.

To spicy groves where he had won
  His plumage of resplendent hue,
His native fruits and skies and sun,
  He bade adieu.

For these he changed the smoke of turf,
  A heathery land and misty sky,
And turn'd on rocks and raging surf
  His golden eye.

But, petted, in our climate cold
  He lived and chatter'd many a day;
Until with age from green and gold
  His wings grew gray.

At last, when blind and seeming dumb,
  He scolded, laughed, and spoke no more,
A Spanish stranger chanced to come
  To Mulla's shore;

He hailed the bird in Spanish speech;
  The bird in Spanish speech replied,
Flapped round his cage with joyous screech,
  Dropt down, and died.

THOMAS CAMPBELL [1777–1844]

TO THE MOCKING BIRD

Who shall thy gay buffoonery describe?
Winged mimic of the woods! thou motley fool!
Thine ever ready notes of ridicule
Pursue thy fellows still with jest and jibe.
Wit, sophist, songster, Yorick of thy tribe,
Thou sportive satirist of Nature's school,
To thee the palm of scoffing we ascribe,
Arch-mocker and mad Abbot of Misrule!
For such thou art by day – but all night long
Thou pourest a soft, sweet, pensive, solemn strain,
As if thou didst in this thy moonlight song
Like to the melancholy Jacques complain,
Musing on falsehood, folly, vice and wrong,
And sighing for thy motley coat again.

RICHARD HENRY WILDE [1789–1847]

THE GREEN LINNET

Beneath these fruit-tree boughs that shed
Their snow-white blossoms on my head,
With brightest sunshine round me spread
    Of spring's unclouded weather,
In this sequestered nook how sweet
To sit upon my orchard-seat!
And birds and flowers once more to greet,
    My last year's friends together.

One have I marked, the happiest guest
In all this covert of the blest:
Hail to Thee, far above the rest
    In joy of voice and pinion!
Thou, Linnet! in thy green array,
Presiding Spirit here to-day,
Dost lead the revels of the May;
    And this is thy dominion.

While birds, and butterflies, and flowers,
Make all one band of paramours,
Thou, ranging up and down the bowers,
    Art sole in thy employment:
A Life, a Presence like the Air,
Scattering thy gladness without care,
Too blest with any one to pair;
    Thyself thy own enjoyment.

Amid yon tuft of hazel trees,
That twinkle to the gusty breeze,
Behold him perched in ecstasies,
    Yet seeming still to hover;
There! where the flutter of his wings
Upon his back and body flings
Shadows and sunny glimmerings,
    That cover him all over.

My dazzled sight he oft deceives,
A Brother of the dancing leaves;
Then flits, and from the cottage-eaves
    Pours forth his song in gushes;
As if by that exulting strain
He mocked and treated with disdain
The voiceless Form he chose to feign,
    While fluttering in the bushes.

THOMAS HARDY [1840–1928]

THE OUSEL-COCK SO BLACK OF HUE

from: A Midsummer Night's Dream

The ousel-cock, so black of hue,
    With orange-tawny bill,
The throstle with his note so true,
    The wren with little quill;
The finch, the sparrow, and the lark,
    The plain-song cuckoo gray,
Whose note full many a man doth mark,
    And dares not answer nay.

WILLIAM SHAKESPEARE [1564–1616]

'O NIGHTINGALE...'

O nightingale, that on yon bloomy Spray
  Warbl'st at eeve, when all the Woods are still,
  Thou with fresh hope the Lovers heart dost fill,
  While the jolly hours lead on propitious *May*,
Thy liquid notes that close the eye of Day,
  First heard before the shallow Cuccoo's bill
  Portend success in love; O if *Jove's* will
  Have linkt that amorous power to thy soft lay,
Now timely sing, ere the rude Bird of Hate
  Foretell my hopeless doom in som Grove ny:
  As thou from year to year hast sung too late
For my relief; yet hadst no reason why,
  Whether the Muse, or Love call thee his mate,
  Both them I serve, and of their train am I.

JOHN MILTON [1608–1674]

45

TO A SEA-BIRD

Sauntering hither on listless wings,
  Careless vagabond of the sea,
Little thou heedest the surf that sings,
The bar that thunders, the shale that rings, –
  Give me to keep thy company.

Little thou hast, old friend, that's new;
  Storms and wrecks are old things to thee;
Sick am I of these changes, too;
Little to care for, little to rue, –
  I on the shore, and thou on the sea.

All of thy wanderings, far and near,
  Bring thee at last to shore and me;
All of my journeyings end them here,
This our tether must be our cheer, –
  I on the shore, and thou on the sea.

Lazily rocking on ocean's breast,
  Something in common, old friend, have we;
Thou on the shingle seek'st thy nest,
I to the waters look for rest, –
  I on the shore, and thou on the sea.

BRET HARTE [1836–1902]

46

TO A SKYLARK

Hail to thee, blithe spirit!
  Bird thou never wert –
That from heaven or near it
  Pourest thy full heart
In profuse strains of unpremeditated art.

Higher still and higher
  From the earth thou springest,
Like a cloud of fire;
  The blue deep thou wingest,
And singing still dost soar, and soaring ever singest.

In the golden light'ning
  Of the sunken sun
O'er which clouds are bright'ning
  Thou dost float and run,
Like an unbodied joy whose race is just begun.

The pale purple even
  Melts around thy flight;
Like a star of heaven,
  In the broad daylight
Thou art unseen, but yet I hear thy shrill delight –

Keen as are the arrows
  Of that silver sphere
Whose intense lamp narrows
  In the white dawn clear,
Until we hardly see, we feel that it is there.

All the earth and air
  With thy voice is loud
As, when night is bare,
  From one lonely cloud
The moon rains out her beams, and heaven is overflow'd.

What thou art we know not;
  What is most like thee?
From rainbow clouds there flow not
  Drops so bright to see,
As from thy presence showers a rain of melody: –

Like a poet hidden
  In the light of thought,
Singing hymns unbidden,
  Till the world is wrought
To sympathy with hopes and fears it heeded not:

Like a high-born maiden
  In a palace tower,
Soothing her love-laden
  Soul in secret hour
With music sweet as love, which overflows her bower:

Like a glow-worm golden
  In a dell of dew,
Scattering unbeholden
  Its aërial hue
Among the flowers and grass which screen it from the view:

Like a rose embower'd
    In its own green leaves,
By warm winds deflower'd,
    Till the scent it gives
Makes faint with too much sweet these heavy-wingèd thieves:

Sound of vernal showers
    On the twinkling grass,
Rain-awaken'd flowers –
    All that ever was
Joyous and clear and fresh – thy music doth surpass.

Teach us, sprite or bird,
    What sweet thoughts are thine:
I have never heard
    Praise of love or wine
That panted forth a flood of rapture so divine.

Chorus hymeneal,
    Or triumphal chant,
Match'd with thine would be all
    But an empty vaunt –
A thing wherein we feel there is some hidden want.

What objects are the fountains
    Of thy happy strain?
What fields, or waves, or mountains?
    What shapes of sky or plain?
What love of thine own kind? what ignorance of pain?

With thy clear keen joyance
    Languor cannot be:
Shadow of annoyance
    Never came near thee:
Thou lovest, but ne'er knew love's sad satiety.

Waking or asleep,
    Thou of death must deem
Things more true and deep
    Than we mortals dream,
Or how could thy notes flow in such a crystal stream?

We look before and after,
    And pine for what is not:
Our sincerest laughter
    With some pain is fraught;
Our sweetest songs are those that tell of saddest thought.

Yet, if we could scorn
    Hate and pride and fear,
If we were things born
    Not to shed a tear,
I know not how thy joy we ever should come near.

Better than all measures
    Of delightful sound,
Better than all treasures
    That in books are found,
Thy skill to poet were, thou scorner of the ground!

Teach me half the gladness
    That thy brain must know;
Such harmonious madness
    From my lips would flow,
The world should listen then, as I am listening now.

PERCY BYSSHE SHELLEY [1792–1822]

SWEET SUFFOLKE OWLE

Sweet Suffolke Owle, so trimly dight,
With feathers like a Lady bright,
Thou sing'st alone, sitting, by night,
    Te whit, te whoo,
Thy note that forth so freely roules,
With shrill command the Mouse controules,
And sings a dirge for dying soules,
    Te whit, te whoo.

ANONYMOUS

THE MOCKING BIRD

Superb and sole, upon a plumèd spray
That o'er the general leafage boldly grew
He summ'd the woods in song; or typic drew
The watch of hungry hawks, the lone dismay
Of languid doves when long their lovers stray
And all birds' passion-plays that sprinkle dew
At morn in brake or bosky avenue.
Whate'er birds did or dreamed, this bird could say.
Then down he shot, bounced airily along
The sward, twitched in grasshopper, made song
Midflight, perched, prinked, and to his art again.
Sweet Science, this large riddle read me plain:
How may the death of that dull insect be
The life of yon trim Shakespeare on the tree?

SIDNEY LANIER [1842–1881]

TWO PEWITS

Under the after-sunset sky
Two pewits sport and cry,
More white than is the moon on high
Riding the dark surge silently;
More black than earth. Their cry
Is the one sound under the sky.
They alone move, now low, now high,
And merrily they cry
To the mischievous Spring sky,
Plunging earthward, tossing high,
Over the ghost who wonders why
So merrily they cry and fly,
Nor choose 'twixt earth and sky,
While the moon's quarter silently
Rides, and earth rests as silently.

EDWARD THOMAS [1878–1917]

THE DARKLING THRUSH

I leant upon a coppice gate
    When Frost was spectre-gray,
And Winter's dregs made desolate
    The weakening eye of day.
The tangled bine-stems scored the sky
    Like strings of broken lyres,
And all mankind that haunted nigh
    Had sought their household fires.

The land's sharp features seemed to be
    The Century's corpse outleant,
His crypt the cloudy canopy,
    The wind his death-lament.
The ancient pulse of germ and birth
    Was shrunken hard and dry,
And every spirit upon earth
    Seemed fervourless as I.

At once a voice arose among
    The bleak twigs overhead
In a full-hearted evensong
    Of joy illimited;
An aged thrush, frail, gaunt, and small,
    In blast-beruffled plume,
Had chosen thus to fling his soul
    Upon the growing gloom.

So little cause for carolings
    Of such ecstatic sound
Was written on terrestrial things
    Afar or nigh around,
That I could think there trembled through
    His happy good-night air
Some blessed Hope, whereof he knew
    And I was unaware.

THOMAS HARDY [1840–1928]

THE KINGFISHER

from: Upon Appleton House

So when the shadows laid asleep
From underneath these banks do creep,
And on the river as it flows
With ebon shuts begin to close;
The modest Halcyon comes in sight,
Flying betwixt the day and night;
And such an horror calm and dumb,
Admiring Nature does benumb.

The viscous air, wheresoe'er she fly,
Follows and sucks her azure dye;
The jellying stream compacts below,
If it might fix her shadow so;
The stupid fishes hang, as plain
As flies in crystal overta'en;
And men the silent scene assist,
Charm'd with the sapphire-wingèd mist.

ANDREW MARVELL [1621–1678]

TO THE CUCKOO

O blithe New-comer! I have heard,
I hear thee and rejoice.
O Cuckoo! shall I call thee Bird,
Or but a wandering Voice?

While I am lying on the grass
Thy twofold shout I hear,
From hill to hill it seems to pass,
At once far off, and near.

Though babbling only to the Vale,
Of sunshine and of flowers,
Thou bringest unto me a tale
Of visionary hours.

Thrice welcome, darling of the Spring!
Even yet thou art to me
No bird, but an invisible thing,
A voice, a mystery;

The same whom in my school-boy days
I listened to; that Cry
Which made me look a thousand ways
In bush, and tree, and sky.

To seek thee did I often rove
Through woods and on the green;
And thou wert still a hope, a love;
Still longed for, never seen.

And I can listen to thee yet;
Can lie upon the plain
And listen, till I do beget
That golden time again.

O blessèd Bird! the earth we pace
Again appears to be
An unsubstantial, faery place;
That is fit home for Thee!

WILLIAM WORDSWORTH [1770–1850]

SPEAK, PARROT

My name is Parrot, a bird of Paradise,
   By nature devised of a wonderous kind,
Daintily dieted with divers delicate spice
   Till Euphrates, that flood, driveth me into Ind;
   Where men of that countrý by fortune me find
And send me to greatè ladyès of estate:
Then Parrot must have an almond or a date.

A cage curiously carven, with a silver pin,
   Properly painted, to be my coverture;
A mirror of glassè, that I may toot therein:
   These, maidens full meekly with many a divers flower,
   Freshly they dress, and makè sweet my bower,
With 'Speak, Parrot, I pray you!' full curtesly they say,
'Parrot is a goodly bird, a pretty popinjay!'

With my bekè bent, my little wanton eye,
   My feathers fresh as is the emerald green,
About my neck a circulet like the rich rubý,
   My little leggès, my feet both feat and clean,
   I am a minion to wait upon a queen.
'My proper Parrot, my little pretty fool!'
With ladies I learn, and go with them to school.

'Ha! Ha! Ha! Parrot, ye can laugh prettily!'
   Parrot hath not dinéd all this long day.
Like your puss-cat, Parrot can mew and cry
   In Latin, Hebrew, Araby and Chaldy;
   In Greekė tongue Parrot can both speak and say,
As Persius, that poet, doth report of me,
'Quis expedivit psittaco suum chaire?'*

JOHN SKELTON [1460–1529]

*Who taught Parrot to say 'Hallo!'?

THE PUZZLED GAME BIRDS

They are not those who used to feed us
When we were young – they cannot be –
These shapes that now bereave and bleed us?
They are not those who used to feed us,
For did we then cry, they would heed us.
– If hearts can house such treachery
They are not those who used to feed us
When we were young – they cannot be!

THOMAS HARDY [1840–1928]

CORNCRAKES

Incorrigible, unmusical,
They bridged the surrounding hedge of my childhood,
Unsubtle, the opposite of blackbirds,
But, unlike blackbirds, capable
Anywhere they are of endorsing summer
Like loud men around the corner
Whom we never see but whose raucous
Voices can give us confidence.

LOUIS MACNEICE [1907–1963]

THE SELFSAME SONG

A bird sings the selfsame song,
With never a fault in its flow,
That we listened to here those long
    Long years ago.

A pleasing marvel is how
A strain of such rapturous rote
Should have gone on thus till now
    Unchanged in a note!

– But it's not the selfsame bird. –
No: perished to dust is he . . .
As also are those who heard
    That song with me.

THOMAS HARDY [1840–1928]

THE BLACKBIRD

O Blackbird! sing me something well:
   While all the neighbours shoot thee round,
   I keep smooth plats of fruitful ground,
Where thou may'st warble, eat and dwell.

The espaliers and the standards all
   Are thine; the range of lawn and park:
   The unnetted black-hearts ripen dark,
All thine, against the garden wall.

Yet, tho' I spared thee all the spring,
   Thy sole delight is, sitting still,
   With that gold dagger of thy bill
To fret the summer jenneting.

A golden bill! the silver tongue,
   Cold February loved, is dry:
   Plenty corrupts the melody
That made thee famous once, when young:

And in the sultry garden-squares,
   Now thy flute-notes are changed to coarse,
   I hear thee not at all, or hoarse
As when a hawker hawks his wares.

Take warning! he that will not sing
   While yon sun prospers in the blue,
   Shall sing for want, ere leaves are new,
Caught in the frozen palms of Spring.

LORD TENNYSON [1809–1892]

THE OWL

When cats run home and light is come,
    And dew is cold upon the ground,
And the far-off stream is dumb,
    And the whirring sail goes round,
    And the whirring sail goes round;
        Alone and warming his five wits,
        The white owl in the belfry sits.

When merry milkmaids click the latch,
    And rarely smells the new-mown hay,
And the cock hath sung beneath the thatch
    Twice or thrice his roundelay,
    Twice or thrice his roundelay;
        Alone and warming his five wits,
        The white owl in the belfry sits.

LORD TENNYSON [1809–1892]

TO THE OWL

Grave Bird, that shelter'd in thy lonely bower,
　　On some tall oak with ivy overspread,
　　Or in some silent barn's deserted shed,
　　Or mid the fragments of some ruin'd tower,
Still, as of old, at this sad solemn hour,
　　When now the toiling Sons of Care are fled,
　　And the freed Ghost slips from his wormy bed,
　　Complaineth loud of Man's ungentle power,
That drives thee from the cheerful face of day
　　To tell thy sorrows to the pale-eyed Night,
　　Like thee, escaping from the sunny ray,
I woo this gloom, to hide me from the sight
　　Of that fell Tribe whose persecuting sway
　　On Me and Thee alike is bent to light.

THOMAS RUSSELL [1762–1788]

69

TURKEYS

The turkeys wade the close to catch the bees
In the old border full of maple trees
And often lay away and breed and come
And bring a brood of chelping chickens home.
The turkey gobbles loud and drops his rag
And struts and sprunts his tail and then lets drag
His wing on ground and makes a huzzing noise,
Nauntles at passer-bye and drives the boys
And bounces up and flies at passer-bye.
The old dog snaps and grins nor ventures nigh.
He gobbles loud and drives the boys from play;
They throw their sticks and kick and run away.

JOHN CLARE [1793–1864]

THE THRUSH'S NEST

Within a thick and spreading hawthorn bush,
   That overhung a molehill large and round,
I heard from morn to morn a merry thrush
   Sing hymns to sunrise, and I drank the sound
With joy; and, often an intruding guest,
   I watched her secret toils from day to day –
How true she warped the moss, to form a nest,
   And modelled it within with wood and clay;
And by and by, like heath-bells gilt with dew,
   There lay her shining eggs, as bright as flowers,
Ink-spotted-over shells of greeny blue;
   And there I witnessed in the sunny hours
A brood of nature's minstrels chirp and fly,
Glad as that sunshine and the laughing sky.

JOHN CLARE [1793–1864]

PROUD SONGSTERS

The thrushes sing as the sun is going,
    And the finches whistle in ones and pairs,
And as it gets dark loud nightingales
       In bushes
Pipe, as they can when April wears,
    As if all Time were theirs.

These are brand-new birds of twelve-months' growing,
Which a year ago, or less than twain,
No finches were, nor nightingales,
       Nor thrushes,
But only particles of grain,
    And earth, and air, and rain.

THOMAS HARDY [1840–1928]

73

THE THRUSH

When Winter's ahead,
What can you read in November
That you read in April
When Winter's dead?

I hear the thrush, and I see
Him alone at the end of the lane
Near the bare poplar's tip,
Singing continuously.

Is it more that you know
Than that, even as in April,
So in November,
Winter is gone that must go?

Or is all your lore
Not to call November November,
And April April,
And Winter Winter – no more?

But I know the months all,
And their sweet names, April,
May and June and October,
As you call and call

I must remember
What died in April
And consider what will be born
Of a fair November;

And April I love for what
It was born of, and November
For what it will die in,
What they are and what they are not,

While you love what is kind,
What you can sing in
And love and forget in
All that's ahead and behind.

EDWARD THOMAS [1878–1917]

The
CREATION
—— of ——
BEASTS

THE CREATION OF BEASTS

from: Paradise Lost (Book VII)

The Sixt, and of Creation last arose
With Eevning Harps and Mattin, when God said,
Let th' Earth bring forth Soul living in her kinde,
Cattle and Creeping things, and Beast of the Earth,
Each in their kinde. The Earth obey'd, and strait
Op'ning her fertil Woomb teem'd at a Birth
Innumerous living Creatures, perfet formes,
Limb'd and full grown: out of the ground up rose
As from his Laire the wilde Beast where he wonns
In Forrest wilde, in Thicket, Brake, or Den;
Among the Trees in Pairs they rose, they walk'd:
The Cattel in the Fields and Meddowes green;
Those rare and solitarie, these in flocks
Pasturing at once, and in broad Herds upsprung.
The grassie Clods now Calv'd, now half appeer'd
The Tawnie Lion, pawing to get free
His hinder parts, then springs as broke from Bonds,
And Rampant shakes his Brinded main; the Ounce,
The Libbard, and the Tyger, as the Moale
Rising, the crumbl'd Earth above them threw
In Hillocks; the swift Stag from under ground
Bore up his branching head: scarse from his mould
Behemoth *biggest born of Earth upheav'd*
His vastness: Fleec't the Flocks and bleating rose,
As Plants: ambiguous between Sea and Land
The River Horse and scalie Crocodile.

JOHN MILTON [1608–1674]

79

ANIMALS' SENSES

from: Essay on Man

What modes of sight betwixt each wide extreme,
The mole's dim curtain, and the lynx's beam:
Of smell, the headlong lioness between,
And hound sagacious on the tainted green:
Of hearing, from the life that fills the flood,
To that which warbles thro' the vernal wood?
The spider's touch, how exquisitely fine!
Feels at each thread, and lives along the line:
In the nice bee, what sense so subtly true
From pois'nous herbs extracts the healing dew?
How Instinct varies in the grov'ling swine,
Compar'd, half-reas'ning elephant, with thine!

ALEXANDER POPE [1688–1744]

THE BULL

from: The Seasons

Through all his lusty veins
The bull, deep-scorch'd, the raging passion feels.
Of pasture sick, and negligent of food,
Scarce seen, he wades among the yellow broom,
While o'er his ample sides the rambling sprays
Luxuriant shoot; or through the mazy wood
Dejected wanders, nor th' enticing bud
Crops, though it presses on his careless sense.
And oft, in jealous madd'ning fancy wrapt,
He seeks the fight; and, idly-butting, feigns
His rival gor'd in every knotty trunk.
Him should he meet, the bellowing war begins:
Their eyes flash fury; to the hollow'd earth,
Whence the sand flies, they mutter bloody deeds,
And groaning deep, th' impetuous battle mix:
While the fair heifer, balmy-breathing, near,
Stands kindling up their rage.

JAMES THOMSON [1700–1748]

THE OLD BULL

from: The Fable of a Cock and a Bull

A bull, who'd listen'd to the vows
Of above fifteen hundred cows;
And serv'd his master fresh and fresh,
With hecatombs of special flesh,
Like to an hermit or a dervise,
(Grown old and feeble in the service)
Now left the meadow's green parade,
And sought a solitary shade.
The cows proclaim'd in mournful lowing,
The bull's deficiency in wooing,
And to their disappointed master,
All told the terrible disaster.
   'Is this the case' (quoth Hodge) 'O rare!
But hold, to morrow is the fair.
Thou to thy doom, old boy, art fated,
To morrow – and thou shalt be baited.'

CHRISTOPHER SMART [1722–1771]

IN PRAISE OF ANIMALS

from: Jubilate Agno

Let Joshua praise God with an Unicorn – the swift-
   ness of the Lord, and the strength of the Lord, and
   the spear of the Lord mighty in battle.
Let Caleb with an Ounce praise the Lord of the Land
   of beauty and rejoice in the blessing of his good
   Report.
Let Othniel praise God with the Rhinoceros, who put
   on his armour for the reward of beauty in the Lord.
Let Tola bless with the Toad, which is the good
   creature of God, tho' his virtue is in the secret, and
   his mention is not made.
Let Barak praise with the Pard – and great is the
   might of the faithful and great is the Lord in the
   nail of Jael and in the sword of the Son of Abinoam.
Let Gideon bless with the Panther – the Word of the
   Lord is invincible by him that lappeth from the
   brook.
Let Jotham praise with the Urchin, who took up his
   parable and provided himself for the adversary to
   kick against the pricks.
Let Boaz, the Builder of Judah, bless with the Rat,
   which dwelleth in hardship and peril, that they may
   look to themselves and keep their houses in order.
Let Obed-Edom with a Dormouse praise the Name of
   the Lord God his Guest for increase of his store
   and for peace.
Let Abishai bless with the Hyæna – the terror of the
   Lord, and the fierceness of his wrath against the
   foes of the King and of Israel.

Let Ithiel bless with the Baboon, whose motions are
    regular in the wilderness, and who defendeth him-
    self with a staff against the assailant.
Let Ucal bless with the Cameleon, which feedeth on
    the Flowers and washeth himself in the dew.
Let Lemuel bless with the Wolf, which is a dog with-
    out a master, but the Lord hears his cries and feeds
    him in the desert.
Let Hananiah bless with the Civet, which is pure
    from benevolence.
Let Azarias bless with the Reindeer, who runneth
    upon the waters, and wadeth thro' the land in snow.
Let Mishael bless with the Stoat – the praise of the
    Lord gives propriety to all things.

Let Savaran bless with the Elephant, who gave his life
for his country that he might put on immortality.
Let Nehemiah the imitator of God bless with the
Monkey, who is workd down from Man.
Let Manasses bless with the Wild-Ass – liberty beget-
teth insolence, but necessity is the mother of
prayer.
Let Jebus bless with the Camelopard, which is good
to carry and to parry and to kneel.
Let Huz bless with the Polypus – lively subtlety is
acceptable to the Lord.
Let Buz bless with the Jackall – but the Lord is the
Lion's provider.

CHRISTOPHER SMART [1722–1771]

COYOTE

Blown out of the prairie in twilight and dew,
Half bold and half timid, yet lazy all through;
Loth ever to leave, and yet fearful to stay,
He limps in the clearing, – an outcast in grey.

A shade on the stubble, a ghost by the wall,
Now leaping, now limping, now risking a fall,
Lop-eared and large-jointed, but ever alway
A thoroughly vagabond outcast in grey.

Here, Carlo, old fellow, – he's one of your kind, –
Go, seek him, and bring him in out of the wind.
What! snarling, my Carlo! So – even dogs may
Deny their own kin in the outcast in grey.

Well, take what you will, – though it be on the sly,
Marauding, or begging, – I shall not ask why;
But will call it a dole, just to help on his way
A four-footed friar in orders of grey!

BRET HARTE [1836–1902]

THE FROG

The Frog by Nature is both damp and cold,
Her mouth is large, her Belly much will
   hold:
She sits somewhat ascending, loves to be
Croaking in Gardens, though unpleasantly....

JOHN BUNYAN [1628–1688]

THE SQUIRREL

Whisky, frisky,
Hippity hop;
Up he goes
To the tree top!

Whirly, twirly,
Round and round,
Down he scampers
To the ground.

Furly, curly
What a tail!
Tall as a feather
Broad as a sail!

Where's his supper?
In the shell,
Snippity, crackity,
Out it fell.

ANONYMOUS

MY CAT JEOFFRY

from: Rejoice in the Lamb

For I will consider my cat Jeoffry.

For he is the servant of the living God, duly and daily serving him.

For at the first glance of the glory of God in the East he worships in his way.

For this is done by wreathing his body seven times round with elegant quickness.

For when he leaps up to catch the musk, which is the blessing of God upon his prayer.

For he rolls upon prank to work it in.

For having done duty and received blessing he begins to consider himself.

For this he performs in ten degrees.

For first he looks upon his fore-paws to see if they are clean.

For secondly he kicks up behind to clear away there.

For thirdly he works it upon stretch with the fore-paws extended.

For fourthly he sharpens his paws by wood.

For fifthly he washes himself.

For sixthly he rolls upon wash.

For seventhly he fleas himself, that he may not be interrupted upon the beat.

For eighthly he rubs himself against a post.

For ninthly he looks up for his instructions.

For tenthly he goes in quest of food.

For having consider'd God and himself he will consider his neighbour.

For if he meets another cat he will kiss her in kindness.

For when he takes his prey he plays with it to give it [a] chance.

For one mouse in seven escapes by his dallying.

For when his day's work is done his business more properly
begins.
For he keeps the Lord's watch in the night against the
adversary.
For he counteracts the powers of darkness by his electrical
skin and glaring eyes.
For he counteracts the Devil, who is death, by brisking about
the life.

For in his morning orisons he loves the sun and the sun loves
him.
For he is of the tribe of Tiger.
For the Cherub Cat is a term of the Angel Tiger.
For he has the subtlety and hissing of a serpent, which in
goodness he suppresses.
For he will not do destruction, if he is well-fed, neither will
he spit without provocation.

For he purrs in thankfulness, when God tells him he's a good
    Cat.
For he is an instrument for the children to learn benevolence
    upon.
For every house is incomplete without him & a blessing is
    lacking in the spirit.
For the Lord commanded Moses concerning the cats at the
    departure of the Children of Israel from Egypt.
For every family had one cat at least in the bag.
For the English cats are the best in Europe.
For he is the cleanest in the use of his fore-paws of any
    quadrupeds.
For the dexterity of his defence is an instance of the love of
    God to him exceedingly.
For he is the quickest to his mark of any creature.
For he is tenacious of his point.
For he is a mixture of gravity and waggery.
For he knows that God is his Saviour.
For there is nothing sweeter than his peace when at rest.
For there is nothing brisker than his life when in motion.
For he is of the Lord's poor and so indeed is he called by
    benevolence perpetually – Poor Jeoffry! poor Jeoffry! the
    rat has bit thy throat.
For I bless the name of the Lord Jesus that Jeoffry is better.
For the divine spirit comes about his body to sustain it in
    compleat cat.
For his tongue is exceeding pure so that it has in purity what
    it wants in musick.
For he is docile and can learn certain things.
For he can set up with gravity which is patience upon
    approbation.

For he can fetch and carry, which is patience in employment.
For he can jump over a stick which is patience upon proof
    positive.
For he can spraggle upon waggle at the word of command.
For he can jump from an eminence into his master's bosom.
For he can catch the cork and toss it again.
For he is hated by the hypocrite and miser.
For the former is afraid of detection.
For the latter refused the charge.
For he camels his back to bear the first motion of business.
For he is good to think on, if a man would express himself
    neatly.
For he made a great figure in Egypt for his signal services.
For he killed the Icneumon-rat very pernicious by land.

For his ears are so acute that they sting again.
For from this proceeds the passing quickness of his attention.
For by stroaking of him I have found out electricity.
For I perceived God's light about him both wax and fire.
For the Electrical fire is the spiritual substance, which God
    sends from heaven to sustain the bodies both of man and
    beast.
For God has blessed him in the variety of his movements.
For, tho he cannot fly, he is an excellent clamberer.
For his motions upon the face of the earth are more than
    other quadrupeds.
For he can tread to all the measures upon the musick.
For he can swim for life.
For he can creep.

CHRISTOPHER SMART [1722–1771]

THE RAT

The rat is the concisest tenant.
He pays no rent, –
Repudiates the obligation,
On schemes intent.

Balking our wit
To sound or circumvent,
Hate cannot harm
A foe so reticent.

Neither decree
Prohibits him,
Lawful as
Equilibrium.

EMILY DICKINSON [1830–1886]

EPITAPH ON A HARE

Here lies, whom hound did ne'er pursue,
   Nor swifter greyhound follow,
Whose foot ne'er tainted morning dew,
   Nor ear heard huntsman's hallo',

Old Tiney, surliest of his kind,
   Who, nurs'd with tender care,
And to domestic bounds confin'd,
   Was still a wild Jack-hare.

Though duly from my hand he took
   His pittance ev'ry night,
He did it with a jealous look,
   And, when he could, would bite.

His diet was of wheaten bread,
   And milk, and oats, and straw,
Thistles, or lettuces instead,
   With sand to scour his maw.

On twigs of hawthorn he regal'd,
   On pippins' russet peel;
And, when his juicy salads fail'd,
   Slic'd carrot pleas'd him well.

A Turkey carpet was his lawn,
   Whereon he lov'd to bound,
To skip and gambol like a fawn,
   And swing his rump around.

His frisking was at evening hours,
   For then he lost his fear;
But most before approaching show'rs,
   Or when a storm drew near.

Eight years and five round-rolling moons
  He thus saw steal away,
Dozing out all his idle noons,
  And ev'ry night at play.

I kept him for his humour' sake,
  For he would oft beguile
My heart of thoughts that made it ache,
  And force me to a smile.

But now, beneath this walnut-shade
  He finds his long, last home,
And waits in snug concealment laid,
  'Till gentler Puss shall come.

He, still more aged, feels the shocks
  From which no care can save,
And, partner once of Tiney's box,
  Must soon partake his grave.

WILLIAM COWPER [1731–1800]

97

THE RETIRED CAT

A poet's cat, sedate and grave,
As poet well could wish to have,
Was much addicted to inquire
For nooks, to which she might retire,
And where, secure as mouse in chink,
She might repose, or sit and think.
I know not where she caught the trick –
Nature perhaps herself had cast her
In such a mould PHILOSOPHIQUE,
Or else she learn'd it of her master.
Sometimes ascending, debonair,
An apple-tree or lofty pear,
Lodg'd with convenience in the fork,
She watched the gard'ner at his work;
Sometimes her ease and solace sought
In an old empty wat'ring pot,
There wanting nothing, save a fan,
To seem some nymph in her sedan,
Apparell'd in exactest sort,
And ready to be borne to court.

But love of change it seems has place
Not only in our wiser race;
Cats also feel as well as we
That passion's force, and so did she.
Her climbing, she began to find,
Expos'd her too much to the wind,
And the old utensil of tin
Was cold and comfortless within:
She therefore wish'd instead of those,
Some place of more serene repose,
Where neither cold might come, nor air
Too rudely wanton with her hair,
And sought it in the likeliest mode
Within her master's snug abode.

A draw'r, – it chanc'd, at bottom lin'd
With linen of the softest kind,

With such as merchants introduce
From India, for the ladies' use, –
A draw'r impending o'er the rest,
Half open in the topmost chest,
Of depth enough, and none to spare,
Invited her to slumber there.
Puss with delight beyond expression,
Survey'd the scene, and took possession.
Recumbent at her ease ere long,
And lull'd by her own hum-drum song,
She left the cares of life behind,
And slept as she would sleep her last,
When in came, housewifely inclin'd,
The chambermaid, and shut it fast,
By no malignity impell'd,
But all unconscious whom it held.
    Awaken'd by the shock (cried puss)
Was ever cat attended thus!
The open draw'r was left, I see,
Merely to prove a nest for me,
For soon as I was well compos'd,
Then came the maid, and it was closed:
How smooth these 'kerchiefs, and how sweet,
O what a delicate retreat!
I will resign myself to rest
Till Sol, declining in the west,
Shall call to supper; when, no doubt,
Susan will come and let me out.
    The evening came, the sun descended,
And puss remain'd still unattended.
The night roll'd tardily away,
(With her indeed 'twas never day)
The sprightly morn her course renew'd,
The evening gray again ensued,
And puss came into mind no more
Than if entomb'd the day before.

With hunger pinch'd and pinch'd for room,
She now presag'd approaching doom,
Not slept a single wink, or purr'd,
Conscious of jeopardy incurr'd.
    That night, by chance, the poet watching,
Heard an inexplicable scratching,
His noble heart went pit-a-pat,
And to himself he said – what's that?
He drew the curtain at his side,
And forth he peep'd, but nothing spied.
Yet, by his ear directed, guess'd
Something imprison'd in the chest,
And doubtful what, with prudent care,
Resolv'd it should continue there.
At length a voice, which well he knew,
A long and melancholy mew,
Saluting his poetic ears,
Consol'd him, and dispell'd his fears;
He left his bed, he trod the floor.
He 'gan in haste the draw'rs explore,
The lowest first, and without stop,
The rest in order to the top.
For 'tis a truth well known to most,
That whatsoever thing is lost,
We seek it, ere it come to light,
In ev'ry cranny but the right.
Forth skipp'd the cat; not now replete
As erst with airy self-conceit,
Nor in her own fond apprehension,
A theme for all the world's attention,
But modest, sober, cur'd of all
Her notions hyberbolical,
And wishing for a place of rest
Any thing rather than a chest.

WILLIAM COWPER [1731–1800]

TO A CAT

Cat! who has pass'd thy grand climacteric,
   How many mice and rats hast in thy days
   Destroy'd? – How many tit bits stolen? Gaze
With those bright languid segments green, and prick
Those velvet ears – but pr'ythee do not stick
   Thy latent talons in me – and upraise
   Thy gentle mew – and tell me all thy frays
Of fish and mice, and rats and tender chick.
Nay, look not down, nor lick thy dainty wrists –
   For all the wheezy asthma, – and for all
Thy tail's tip is nick'd off – and though the fists
   Of many a maid have given thee many a maul,
Still is that fur as soft as when the lists
   In youth thou enter'dst on glass bottled wall.

JOHN KEATS [1795–1821]

WATER-RAT

By the wide lake's margin I mark'd her lie –
    The wide, weird lake where the alders sigh –
A young fair thing, with a shy, soft eye;
    And I deem'd that her thoughts had flown
To her home, and her brethren, and sisters dear,
As she lay there watching the dark, deep mere,
    All motionless, all alone.

Then I heard a noise, as of men and boys,
    And a boisterous troop drew nigh.
Whither now will retreat those fairy feet?
    Where hide till the storm pass by?
One glance – the wild glance of a hunted thing –
She cast beside her; she gave one spring;
And there follow'd a splash and a broadening ring
    On the lake where the alders sigh.

She had gone from the ken of ungentle men!
    Yet scarce did I mourn for that;
For I knew she was safe in her own home then,
And, the danger past, would appear again,
    For she was a water-rat.

C. S. CALVERLEY [1831–1884]

SNAKE

A narrow fellow in the grass
Occasionally rides;
You may have met him, – did you not?
His notice sudden is.

The grass divides as with a comb,
A spotted shaft is seen;
And then it closes at your feet
And opens further on.

He likes a boggy acre,
A floor too cool for corn.
Yet when a child, and barefoot,
I more than once, at morn,

Have passed, I thought, a whip-lash
Unbraiding in the sun, –
When, stooping to secure it,
It wrinkled, and was gone.

Several of nature's people
I know, and they know me;
I feel for them a transport
Of cordiality;

But never met this fellow,
Attended or alone,
Without a tighter breathing,
And zero at the bone.

EMILY DICKINSON [1830–1886]

THE BAT

Lightless, unholy, eldritch thing,
Whose murky and erratic wing
Swoops so sickeningly, and whose
Aspect to the female Muse
Is a demon's, made of stuff
Like tattered, sooty waterproof,
Looking dirty, clammy, cold.

Wicked, poisonous, and old:
I have maligned thee! . . . for the Cat
Lately caught a little bat,
Seized it softly, bore it in.
On the carpet, dark as sin
In the lamplight, painfully
It limped about, and could not fly.

Even fear must yield to love,
And pity makes the depths to move.
Though sick with horror, I must stoop,
Grasp it gently, take it up,
And carry it, and place it where
It could resume the twilight air.

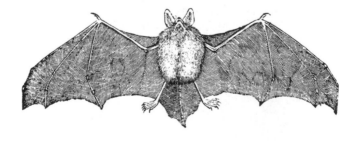

Strange revelation! warm as milk,
Clean as a flower, smooth as silk!
O what a piteous face appears,
What great fine thin translucent ears!
What chestnut down and crapy wings,
Finer than any lady's things –
And O a little one that clings!

Warm, clean, and lovely, though not fair,
And burdened with a mother's care:
Go hunt the hurtful fly, and bear
My blessing to your kind in air.

RUTH PITTER [1897–   ]

THE BAT

The bat is dun with wrinkled wings
    Like fallow article,
And not a song pervades his lips,
    Or none perceptible.

His small umbrella, quaintly halved,
    Describing in the air
An arc alike inscrutable, –
    Elate philosopher!

Deputed from what firmament
    Of what astute abode,
Empowered with what malevolence
    Auspiciously withheld.

To his adroit Creator
    Ascribe no less the praise;
Beneficent, believe me,
    His eccentricities.

EMILY DICKINSON [1830–1886]

OTTER

Would you preserve a num'rous finny race
Let your fierce dog the rav'nous otter chace:
Th' amphibious monster ranges all the shores,
Darts through the waves, and ev'ry haunt explores.
Or let the gin his roving steps betray,
And save from hostile jaws the scaly prey.

JOHN GAY [1685–1732]

THE HUNTED HARE

from: Venus and Adonis

By this, poor Wat*, far off upon a hill,
Stands on his hinder legs with listening ear,
To hearken if his foes pursue him still:
Anon their loud alarums he doth hear;
   And now his grief may be compared well
   To one sore sick that hears the passing-bell.

Then shalt thou see the dew-bedabbled wretch
Turn, and return, indenting with the way;
Each envious briar his weary legs doth scratch,
Each shadow makes him stop, each murmur stay:
   For misery is trodden on by many,
   And being low never relieved by any.

WILLIAM SHAKESPEARE [1564–1616]

*i.e. hare

THE HORSE

from: Henry V

I will not change my horse with any that treads ...
When I bestride him, I soar, I am a hawk.
He trots the air; the earth sings when he touches it.
The basest horn of his hoof is more musical
Than the pipe of Hermes ...
He's of the colour of the nutmeg and of the heat of the ginger ...
He is pure air and fire, and the dull elements
Of earth and water never appear in him,
But only in patient stillness while his rider mounts him ...
It is the prince of palfreys. His neigh is like
The bidding of a monarch, and his countenance
Enforces homage.

WILLIAM SHAKESPEARE [1564–1616]

LYARDE IS AN OLDE HORSE

Lyarde is an olde horse and may nought wel drawe;
He shall be put into the park holyn for the gnawe.
Barefoot withouten shone there shall he go,
For he is an olde horse and may no more do.
Whiles that Lyarde may drawe, the whiles was he loved;
They put him on provande, and therewith he proved.
Now he may nought do his dede and therewith he proved.
Now he may nought do his dede as he might beforn.
Thay lig him before pese-straw, and beres away the corn.
They lede him to the smithy to pulle off his shone
And puttes him to greenwoode, ther for the gone.
Who-so may nought do his dede, he shall to park,
Barefoot wihouten shone, and go with Lyarde.

JOHN LYDGATE [1370?–1451?]

TO A YOUNG ASS

ITS MOTHER BEING TETHERED NEAR IT

Poor little Foal of an oppressèd race!
I love the languid patience of thy face:
And oft with gentle hand I give thee bread,
And clap thy ragged coat and pat thy head.
But what thy dullèd spirits hath dismay'd,
That never thou dost sport along the glade?
And (most unlike the nature of things young)
That earthward still thy moveless head is hung?
Do thy prophetic fears anticipate,
Meek Child of Misery! thy future fate?
The starving meal, and all the thousand aches
'Which patient Merit of the Unworthy takes'?
Or is thy sad heart thrill'd with filial pain
To see thy wretched mother's shorten'd chain?
And truly, very piteous is *her* lot
Chain'd to a log within a narrow spot,
Where the close-eaten grass is scarcely seen,
While sweet around her waves the tempting green.
Poor Ass! thy master should have learnt to show
Pity – best taught by fellowship of Woe!
For much I fear me that *he* lives like thee,
Half famish'd in a land of Luxury!
How *askingly* its footsteps hither bend!
It seems to say, 'And have I then *one* friend?'
Innocent foal! thou poor despis'd forlorn!
I hail thee *Brother* – spite of the fool's scorn!
And fain would take thee with me, in the Dell
Of Peace and mild Equality to dwell,
Where Toil shall call the charmer Health his bride,
And Laughter tickle Plenty's ribless side!

How thou would'st toss thy heels in gamesome play,
And frisk about, as lamb or kitten gay!
Yea! and more musically sweet to me
Thy dissonant harsh bray of joy would be,
Than warbled melodies that soothe to rest
The aching of pale Fashion's vacant breast.

SAMUEL TAYLOR COLERIDGE [1772–1834]

TO A LIZARD

Why run away, poor lizard? why
Art thou so diffident and shy?
Trust to my word; I only want
To look awhile and see thee pant.
For well I know thy pantings are
No signs of sorrow or of care,
Altho' they swell thy jewel'd breast
And never let it lie at rest:
Even when thou sinkest to repose
None ever saw thy eyelids close.
Turn, I beseech thee, turn again,
So mayst thou watch no fly in vain.

WALTER SAVAGE LANDOR [1775–1864]

THE MASTIFFS

from: Fables

Those who in quarrels interpose,
Must often wipe a bloody nose.
A Mastiff, of true English blood,
Lov'd fighting better than his food.
When dogs were snarling for a bone,
He long'd to make the war his own,
And often found (when two contend)
To interpose obtain'd his end;
He glory'd in his limping pace;
The scars of honour seam'd his face;
In ev'ry limb a gash appears,
And frequent fights retrench'd his ears.

    As, on a time, he heard from far
Two dogs engag'd in noisy war,
Away he scours and lays about him,
Resolv'd no fray should be without him.

    Forth from his yard a tanner flies,
And to the bold intruder cries:

    A cudgel shall correct your manners,
Whence sprung this cursed hate to tanners?
While on my dog you vent your spite,
Sirrah! 'tis me you dare not bite.

    To see the battle thus perplex'd,
With equal rage a butcher vex'd,
Hoarse-screaming from the circled crowd,
To the curs'd Mastiff cries aloud:

    Both Hockley-hole and Mary-bone
The combats of my Dog have known.
He ne'er, like bullies coward-hearted,
Attacks in public, to be parted.
Think not, rash fool, to share his fame:
Be his the honour or the shame.

Thus said, they swore, and rav'd like thunder;
They dragg'd their fasten'd dogs asunder;
While clubs and kicks from every side
Rebounded from the Mastiff's hide.
    All reeking now with sweat and blood,
Awhile the parted warriors stood,
Then pour'd upon the meddling foe;
Who, worried, howl'd and sprawl'd below.
He rose; and limping from the fray,
By both sides mangled, sneak'd away.

JOHN GAY [1685–1732]

THE ENGLISH BULL DOG

from: The Fable of the English Bull Dog, Butch Mastiff and Quail

A snub-nos'd dog to fat inclin'd
Of the true hogan mogan kind,
The favourite of an English dame,
Mynheer Van Trumpo was his name;
One morning as he chanc'd to range,
Met honest Towzer on the 'Change;
'And whom have we got here, I beg,'
Quoth he, – and lifted up his leg;
'An English dog can't take an airing,
But foreign scoundrels must be staring.
I'd have your French dogs and your Spanish,
And all your Dutch and all your Danish,
By which our species is confounded,
Be hang'd, be poison'd, or be drowned;
No mercy on the race suspected,
Greyhounds from Italy excepted:
By them my dames ne'er prove big-bellied,
For they, poor toads, are Farrinellied.*
Well, of all dogs it stands confess'd,
Your English bull dogs are the best;

I say it, and will set my hand to't,
Campden records it, and I'll stand to't.
'Tis true we have too much urbanity,
Somewhat o'ercharg'd with soft humanity;
The best things must find food for railing,
And every creature has its failing.'

CHRISTOPHER SMART [1722–1771]

*i.e. castrated (from Farinelli, the castrato singer)

THE CROCODILE

How doth the little crocodile
Improve his shining tail
And pour the waters of the Nile
On every golden scale!

How cheerfully he seems to grin
How neatly spread his claws,
And welcomes little fishes in
With gently smiling jaws.

LEWIS CARROLL [1812–1888]

A CROCODILE

Hard by the lilied Nile I saw
A duskish river-dragon stretched along,
The brown habergeon of his limbs enamelled
With sanguine almerdines and rainy pearl:
And on his back there lay a young one sleeping,
No bigger than a mouse; with eyes like beads,
And a small fragment of its speckled egg
Remaining on its harmless, pulpy snout;
A thing to laugh at, as it gaped to catch
The baulking, merry flies. In the iron jaws
Of the great devil-beast, like a pale soul
Fluttering in rocky hell, lightsomely flew
A snowy troculus, with roseate beak
Tearing the hairy leeches from his throat.

THOMAS LOVELL BEDDOES [1803–1849]

CAGED LION

You are afraid. You do not dare
Up to the Lion to lift your eyes,
And unashamed his beauty share
As once in that lost Paradise.

With fallen cunning lay the snare,
With fearful glee shoot home the bar;
Show him for pence imprisoned there –
In a foul sepulchre a star.

His maned neck of massy girth
Only one Arm in love enfolds:
His beauty humbled to the earth
Only my wrathful God beholds.

RUTH PITTER [1897–   ]

THE HORSE SPEAKS

from: Fables

Were we design'd for daily toil,
To drag the plough-share through the soil,
To sweat in harness through the road,
To groan beneath the carrier's load?
How feeble are the two legg'd kind!
What force is in our nerves combin'd!
Shall then our nobler jaws submit
To foam and champ the galling bit?
Shall haughty man my back bestride?
Shall the sharp spur provoke my side?
Forbid it, heav'ns! Reject the rein;
Your shame, your infamy disdain.
Let him the Lion first control,
And still the Tiger's famish'd growl.
Let us, like them, our freedom claim,
And make him tremble at our name.

JOHN GAY [1685–1732]

THE STALLION

A gigantic beauty of a stallion, fresh and responsive to my
    caresses,
Head high in the forehead, wide between the ears,
Limbs glossy and supple, tail dusting the ground,
Eyes full of sparkling wickedness, ears finely cut, flexibly
    moving.

His nostrils dilate as my heels embrace him,
His well-built limbs tremble with pleasure as we race around
    and return.

WALT WHITMAN [1819–1892]

THE TYGER

Tyger! Tyger! burning bright
In the forests of the night,
What immortal hand or eye
Could frame thy fearful symmetry?

In what distant deeps or skies
Burnt the fire of thine eyes?
On what wings dare he aspire?
What the hand dare sieze the fire?

And what shoulder, & what art,
Could twist the sinews of thy heart?
And when thy heart began to beat,
What dread hand? & what dread feet?

What the hammer? what the chain?
In what furnace was thy brain?
What the anvil? what dread grasp
Dare its deadly terrors clasp?

When the stars threw down their spears,
And water'd heaven with their tears,
Did he smile his work to see?
Did he who made the Lamb make thee?

Tyger! Tyger! burning bright
In the forests of the night,
What immortal hand or eye,
Dare frame thy fearful symmetry?

WILLIAM BLAKE [1797–1827]

KANGAROO

In the northern hemisphere
Life seems to leap at the air, or skim under the wind
Like stags on rocky ground, or pawing horses, or springy
    scut-tailed rabbits.

Or else rush horizontal to charge at the sky's horizon,
Like bulls or bisons or wild pigs.

Or slip like water slippery towards its ends,
As foxes, stoats, and wolves, and prairie dogs.

Only mice, and moles, and rats, and badgers, and beavers,
    and perhaps bears
Seem belly-plumbed to the earth's mid-navel.
Or frogs that when they leap come flop, and flop to the centre
    of the earth.

But the yellow antipodal Kangaroo, when she sits up,
Who can unseat her, like a liquid drop that is heavy, and
    just touches earth.

The downward drip.
The down-urge.
So much denser than cold-blooded frogs.

Delicate mother Kangaroo
Sitting up there rabbit-wise, but huge, plumb-weighted,
And lifting her beautiful slender face, oh! so much more
    gently and finely lined than a rabbit's, or than a hare's,
Lifting her face to nibble at a round white peppermint drop,
    which she loves, sensitive mother Kangaroo.

Her sensitive, long, pure-bred face.
Her full antipodal eyes, so dark,
So big and quiet and remote, having watched so many empty
    dawns in silent Australia.

Her little loose hands, and drooping Victorian shoulders.
And then her great weight below the waist, her vast pale belly
With a thin young yellow little paw hanging out, and
    straggle of a long thin ear, like ribbon,
Like a funny trimming to the middle of her belly, thin little
    dangle of an immature paw, and one thin ear.

Her belly, her big haunches
And in addition, the great muscular python-stretch of
    her tail.

There, she shan't have any more peppermint drops.
So she wistfully, sensitively sniffs the air, and then turns,
    goes off in slow sad leaps

On the long flat skis of her legs,
Steered and propelled by that steel-strong snake of a tail.

Stops again, half turns, inquisitive to look back.
While something stirs quickly in her belly, and a lean little
    face comes out, as from a window,
Peaked and a bit dismayed,

Only to disappear again quickly away from the sight of the
    world, to snuggle down in the warmth,
Leaving the trail of a different paw hanging out.

Still she watches with eternal, cocked wistfulness!
How full her eyes are, like the full, fathomless, shining eyes
    of an Australian black-boy

Who has been lost so many centuries on the margins of
    existence!

She watches with insatiable wistfulness.
Untold centuries of watching for something to come,
For a new signal from life, in that silent lost land of the
     South

Where nothing bites but insects and snakes and the sun,
     small life.
Where no bull roared, no cow ever lowed, no stag cried, no
     leopard screeched, no lion coughed, no dog barked,
But all was silent save for parrots occasionally, in the
     haunted blue bush.

Wistfully watching, with wonderful liquid eyes.
And all her weight, all her blood, dripping sack-wise down
     towards the earth's centre,
And the live little one taking in its paw at the door of her
     belly.

Leap then, and come down on the line that draws to the
     earth's deep, heavy centre.

D. H. LAWRENCE [1885–1930]

SHEPHEARD'S DOGGE

from: The Shepheardes Calendar, September

Thilk same Shepheard mought I well marke;
He has a dogge to byte or to barke;
Never had shepheard so kene a kurre,
That waketh and if but a leafe sturre.
Whilome there wonned a wicked wolfe,
That with many a lambe had glutted his gulfe.
And ever at night wont to repayre
Unto the flocke, when the welkin shone faire,
Ycladde in clothing of seely sheepe,
When the good old man used to sleepe.
Tho at midnight he would barke and ball,
(For he had eft learned a curres call,)
As if a woolfe were emong the sheepe.
With that the shepheard would breake his sleepe,
And send out Lowder (for so his dog hote)
To raunge the fields with wide open throte.
Tho, whenas Lowder was farre awaye,
This wolvish sheepe would catchen his pray ...
At end, the shepheard his practise spyed,
(For Roffy is wise, and as Argus eyed)
And when at even he came to the flocke,
Fast in theyr folds he did them locke, ...
For it was a perilous beast above all,
And eke had he cond the shepherds call,
And oft in the night came to the shepecote,
And called Lowder, with a hollow throte
As if it the old man selfe had bene.

The dog his maisters voice did it weene,
Yet halfe in doubt he opened the dore,
And ranne out, as he was wont of yore.
No sooner was out, but swifter than thought,
Fast by the hyde the wolfe Lowder caught;
And had not Roffy renne to the steven,
Lowder had be slaine thilke same even.

EDMUND SPENSER [1552–1599]

ELEPHANT

from: The Progresse of the Soul

Natures great master-peece, an Elephant,
The onely harmlesse great thing; the giant
Of beasts; who thought, no more had gone, to make one
    wise
But to be just, and thankfull, loth to offend,
(Yet nature hath given him no knees to bend)
Himselfe he up-props, on himselfe relies,
And foe to none, suspects no enemies,
Still sleeping stood; vex't not his fantasie
Blacke dreames; like an unbent bow, carelessly
His sinewy Proboscis did remisly lie.

JOHN DONNE [1573–1631]

THE GARDENER AND THE MOLE

A gardener had watcht a mole
And caught it coming from its hole.
'Mischievous beast!' he cried, 'to harm
The garden as thou dost the farm.
Here thou hast had thy wicked will
Upon my tulip and jonquil.
Behold them drooping and half dead
Upon this torn and tumbled bed.'
   The mole said meekly in reply,
'My star is more to blame than I.
To undermine is mole's commission,
Our house still holds it from tradition.
What lies the nearest us is ours,
Decreed so by the higher Powers.
We hear of conies and of hares,
But when commit we deeds like theirs?
We never touch the flowers that blow,
And only bulbs that lurk below.
'Tis true, where we have run, the ground
Is rais'd a trifle, nor quite sound,
Yet, after a few days of rain,
Level and firm it lies again;
Wise men, like you, will rather wait
For these than argue against fate,
Or quarrel with us moles because
We simply follow Nature's laws.
We raise the turf to keep us warm,
Surely in this there is no harm.
Ye break it up to set thereon
A fortress or perhaps a throne,
And pray that God cast down his eyes
Benignly on burnt sacrifice,
The sacrifice of flesh and bone
Fashioned, they tell us, like His own.

Ye in the cold lie all the night
Under thin tents, at morn to fight.
Neither for horn'd nor fleecy cattle
Start we to mingle in the battle,
Or in the pasture shed their blood
To pamper idleness with food.
Indeed we do eat worms; what then?
Do not those very worms eat men,
And have the impudence to say
Ye shall ere long be such as they?
We never kill or wound a brother,
Men kill by thousands one another,
And, though ye swear ye wish but peace,
Your feuds and warfares never cease.'
   Such homebrought truths the gardener,
Though mild by nature, could not bear,
And lest the mole might more have said
He chopt its head off with the spade.

WALTER SAVAGE LANDOR [1775–1864]

132

UPON THE SNAIL

She goes but softly, but she goeth sure;
  She stumbles not as stronger creatures do:
Her journey's shorter, so she may endure
  Better than they which do much further go.

She makes no noise, but stilly seizeth on
  The flower or herb appointed for her food,
The which she quietly doth feed upon,
  While others range, and gare, but find no good.

And though she doth but very softly go,
  However 'tis not fast, nor slow, but sure;
And certainly they that do travel so,
  The prize they do aim at, they do procure.

JOHN BUNYAN [1628–1688]

GRIZZLY

Coward, – of heroic size,
In whose lazy muscles lies
Strength we fear and yet despise;
Savage, – whose relentless tusks
Are content with acorn husks;
Robber, – whose exploits ne'er soared
O'er the bee's or squirrel's hoard;
Whiskered chin, and feeble nose,
Claws of steel on baby toes, –
Here, in solitude and shade,
Shambling, shuffling, plantigrade,
Be thy courses undismayed!

Here, where Nature makes thy bed,
Let thy rude, half-human tread
   Point to hidden Indian springs,
Lost in ferns and fragrant grasses,
   Hovered o'er by timid wings,
Where the wood-duck lightly passes,
Where the wild bee holds her sweets, –
Epicurean retreats,
Fit for thee, and better than
Fearful spoils of dangerous man.

In thy fat-jowled deviltry
Friar Tuck shall live in thee;
Thou mayst levy tithe and dole;
   Thou shall spread the woodland cheer,
From the pilgrim taking toll;
   Match thy cunning with his fear;
Eat, and drink, and have thy fill;
Yet remain an outlaw still!

BRET HARTE [1836–1902]

134

APE

O lovely O most charming pug
Thy gracefull air & heavenly mug
The beauties of his mind do shine
And every bit is shaped so fine
Your very tail is most devine
Your teeth is whiter then the snow
Yor are a great buck & a bow
Your eyes are of so fine a shape
More like a christians then an ape
His cheeks is like the roses blume
Your hair is like the ravens plume
His noses cast is of the roman
He is a very pretty weomen
I could not get a rhyme for roman
And was oblidged to call it woeman

MARJORY FLEMING [1803–1811]

HEDGEHOG

Twitching the leaves just where the drainpipe clogs
In ivy leaves and mud, a purposeful
Creature at night about its business. Dogs
Fear his stiff seriousness. He chews away

At beetles, worms, slugs, frogs. Can kill a hen
With one snap of his jaws, can taunt a snake
To death on muscled spines. Old countrymen
Tell tales of hedgehogs sucking a cow dry.

But this one, cramped by houses, fences, walls,
Must have slept here all winter in that heap
Of compost, or have inched by intervals
Through tidy gardens to this ivy bed.

And here, dim-eyed, but ears so sensitive
A voice within the house can make him freeze,
He scuffs the edge of danger: yet can live
Happily in our nights and absences.

A country creature, wary, quiet and shrewd,
He takes the milk we give him, when we're gone.
At night, our slamming voices must seem crude
To one who sits and waits for silences.

ANTHONY THWAITE [1930–   ]

FALLOW DEER AT THE LONELY HOUSE

One without looks in to-night
    Through the curtain-chink
From the sheet of glistening white;
One without looks in to-night
    As we sit and think
    By the fender-brink.

We do not discern those eyes
    Watching in the snow;
Lit by lamps of rosy dyes
We do not discern those eyes
    Wondering, aglow,
    Fourfooted, tiptoe.

THOMAS HARDY [1840–1928]

MICE BEFORE MILK

from: The Manciple's Tale

Lat take a cat and fostre hym wel with milk
And tendre flessch and make his couch of silk,
And lat hym seen a mouse go by the wal,
Anon he weyvith milk and flessch and all,
And every deyntee that is in that hous,
Suich appetit he hath to ete a mous.

GEOFFREY CHAUCER [1343–1400]

THE KITTEN

Wanton droll, whose harmless play
Beguiles the rustic's closing day,
When, drawn the evening fire about,
Sit aged crone and thoughtless lout,
And child upon his three-foot stool,
Waiting until his supper cool,
And maid, whose cheek outblooms the rose,
As bright the blazing fagot glows,
Who, bending to the friendly light,
Plies her task with busy sleight;
Come, show thy tricks and sportive graces,
Thus circled round with merry faces!

Backward coil'd and crouching low,
With glaring eyeballs watch thy foe,
The housewife's spindle whirling round,
Or thread or straw that on the ground
Its shadow throws, by urchin sly
Held out to lure thy roving eye;
Then stealing onward, fiercely spring
Upon the tempting faithless thing.
Now, wheeling round with bootless skill,
Thy bo-peep tail provokes thee still,
As still beyond thy curving side
Its jetty tip is seen to glide;
Till from thy centre starting far,
Thou sidelong veerst with rump in air
Erected stiff, and gait awry,
Like madam in her tantrums high;
Though ne'er a madam of them all,
Whose silken kirtle sweeps the hall,
More varied trick and whim displays
To catch the admiring stranger's gaze.

But not alone by cottage fire
Do rustics rude thy feats admire.
The learned sage, whose thoughts explore
The widest range of human lore,

Or with unfetter'd fancy fly
Through airy heights of poesy,
Pausing smiles with alter'd air
To see thee climb his elbow-chair,
Or, struggling on the mat below,
Hold warfare with this slipper'd toe.
The widow'd dame or lonely maid,
Who, in the still but cheerless shade
Of home unsocial, spends her age,
And rarely turns a letter'd page,
Upon her hearth for thee lets fall
The rounded cork or paper ball,
Nor chides thee on thy wicked watch,
The ends of ravell'd skein to catch,
But lets thee have thy wayward will,
Perplexing oft her better skill.

E'en he, whose mind of gloomy bent,
In lonely tower or prison pent,
Reviews the coil of former days,
And loathes the world and all its ways,
Doth power in measured verses dwell,
All thy vagaries wild to tell?
Ah no! the start, the jet, the bound,
The giddy scamper round and round,
With leap and toss and high curvet,
And many a whirling somerset,
(Permitted by the modern muse
Expression technical to use)
These mock the deftest rhymester's skill,
But poor in art, though rich in will.

The featest tumbler, stage bedight,
To thee is but a clumsy wight,
Who every limb and sinew strains
To do what costs thee little pains;
For which, I trow, the gaping crowd
Requite him oft with plaudits loud.

But, stopp'd the while thy wanton play,
Applauses too thy pains repay:
For them, beneath some urchin's hand
With modest pride thou tak'st thy stand,
While many a stroke of kindness glides
Along thy back and tabby sides.
Dilated swells thy glossy fur,
And loudly croons thy busy purr,
As, timing well the equal sound,
Thy clutching feet bepat the ground,
And all their harmless claws disclose
Like prickles of an early rose,
While softly from thy whisker'd cheek
Thy half-closed eyes peer, mild and meek.

What time the lamp's unsteady gleam
Hath roused him from his moody dream,
Feels, as thou gambol'st round his seat,
His heart of pride less fiercely beat,
And smiles, a link in thee to find,
That joins it still to living kind.

Whence hast thou then, thou witless puss!
The magic power to charm us thus?
Is it that in thy glaring eye
And rapid movements, we decry –
Whilst we at ease, secure from ill,
The chimney corner snugly fill –
A lion darting on his prey,
A tiger at his ruthless play?
Or is it that in thee we trace,
With all thy varied wanton grace,
An emblem, view'd with kindred eye,
Of tricky, restless infancy?
Ah! many a lightly sportive child,
Who hath like thee our wits beguiled,
To dull and sober manhood grown,
With strange recoil our hearts disown.

And so, poor kit! must thou endure,
When thou becom'st a cat demure,
Full many a cuff and angry word,
Chased roughly from the tempting board.
But yet, for that thou hast, I ween,
So oft our favour'd play-mate been,
Soft be the change which thou shalt prove!
When time hath spoil'd thee of our love,
Still be thou deem'd by housewife fat
A comely, careful, mousing cat,
Whose dish is, for the public good,
Replenish'd oft with savoury food,
Nor, when thy span of life is past,
Be thou to pond or dung-hill cast,
But, gently borne on goodman's spade,
Beneath the decent sod be laid;
And children show with glistening eyes
The place where poor old pussy lies.

JOANNA BAILLIE [1762–1851]

THE WHALE
from: Paraphrase on Job

At full my huge Leviathan shall rise,
Boast all his strength, and spread his wond'rous size.
Who, great in arms, e'er stripp'd his shining mail,
Or crown'd his triumph with a single scale?
Whose heart sustains him to draw near? behold,
Destruction yawns; his spacious jaws unfold,
And, marshal'd round the wide expanse, disclose
Teeth edg'd with death, and crouding rows on rows.
What hideous fangs on either side arise!
And what a deep abyss between them lies!
Mete with thy lance, and with thy plumbet found,
The one how long, the other how profound.
    His bulk is charg'd with such a furious soul,
That clouds of smoak from his spread nostrils roll,
As from a furnace; and, when rous'd his ire,
Fate issues from his jaws in streams of fire.
The range of tempests, and the roar of seas,
Thy terror, this thy great Superior please;
Strength on his ample shoulders fits in state;
His well join'd limbs are dreadfully complete;
His flakes of solid flesh are slow to part;
As steel his nerves, as adamant his heart.

EDWARD YOUNG [1683–1765]

THE WHALE

from: Paradise Lost (Book I)

Leviathan, which God of all his works
Created hugest that swim th' Ocean stream:
Him haply slumbring on the *Norway* foam
The Pilot of some small night-founder'd Skiff,
Deeming some Island, oft, as Sea-men tell,
With fixed Anchor in his skaly rind
Moors by his side under the Lee, while Night
Invests the Sea, and wished Morn delayes.

JOHN MILTON [1608–1674]

THE WHALE

from: The Loves of the Plants

So, warm and buoyant in his oily mail,
Gambols on seas of ice the unwieldy Whale;
Wide-waving fins round floating island urge
His bulk gigantic through the troubled surge.
With hideous yawn the flying shoals he seeks,
Or clasp with fringe of horn his massy cheeks;
Lifts o'er the tossing wave his nostrils bare,
And spouts pellucid columns into air;
The silvery arches catch the setting beams,
And transient rainbows tremble o'er the streams.

ERASMUS DARWIN [1731–1802)

143

INSCRIPTION ON THE MONUMENT OF A NEWFOUNDLAND DOG

When some proud son of man returns to earth,
Unknown to glory, but upheld by birth,
The sculptor's hand exhausts the pomp of woe
And storied urns record who rest below:
When all is done, upon the tomb is seen,
Not what he was, but what he should have been:
But the poor dog, in life the firmest friend,
The first to welcome, foremost to defend,
Whose honest heart is still his master's own,
Who labours, fights, lives, breathes for him alone.
Unhonour'd fall, unnoticed all his worth,
Denied in heaven the soul he held on earth,
While man, vain insect! hopes to be forgiven,
And claims himself a sole, exclusive heaven.
Oh man! thou feeble tenant of an hour,
Debased by slavery, or corrupt by power,
Who knows thee well must quit thee with disgust,
Degraded mass of animated dust!
Thy love is lust, thy friendship all a cheat,
Thy smiles hypocrisy, thy word deceit!
By nature vile, ennobled but by name,
Each kindred brute might bid thee blush for shame.
Ye! who perchance behold this simple urn,
Pass on – it honours none you wish to mourn:
To mark a friend's remains these stones arise;
I never knew but one, – and here he lies.

LORD BYRON [1788–1824]

B. ESLINGTON 1789   P.VBB

THE SNAIL

To grass, or leaf, or fruit, or wall,
The Snail sticks close, nor fears to fall,
As if he grew there, house and all
                Together.

Within that house secure he hides
When danger imminent betides
Of storms, or other harm besides,
                Of weather.

Give but his horns the slightest touch.
His self-collecting power is such,
He shrinks into his house with much
                Displeasure.

Where'er he dwells, he dwells alone,
Except himself has chattels none,
Well satisfied to be his own
                Whole treasure.

Thus hermit-like, his life he leads,
Nor partner of his Banquet needs,
And if he meets one, only feeds
                The faster.

Who seeks him must be worse than blind
(He and his house are so combined)
If, finding it, he fails to find
                Its master.

WILLIAM COWPER [1731–1800]

THE CHIPMUNK'S DAY

In and out the bushes, up the ivy,
Into the hole
By old oak stump, the chipmunk flashes.
Up the pole

To the feeder full of seeds he dashes,
Stuffs his cheeks,
The chickadee and titmouse scold him.
Down he streaks.

Red as the leaves the wind blows off the maple,
Red as a fox,
Striped like a skunk, the chipmunk whistles
Past the love seat, past the mailbox,

Down the path,
Home to his warm hole stuffed with sweet
Things to eat.
Neat and slight and shining, his front feet

Curled at his breast, he sits there while the sun
Stripes the red west
With its last light: the chipmunk
Dives to his rest.

RANDALL JARRELL [1914–1965]

THE FOX

The shepherd on his journey heard when nigh
His dog among the bushes barking high;
The ploughman ran and gave a hearty shout,
He found a weary fox and beat him out.
The ploughman laughed and would have ploughed him in
But the old shepherd took him for the skin.
He lay upon the furrow stretched for dead,
The old dog lay and licked the wounds that bled,
The ploughman beat him till his ribs would crack,
And then the shepherd slung him at his back;
And when he rested, to his dog's surprise,
The old fox started from his dead disguise;
And while the dog lay panting in the sedge
He up and snapt and bolted through the hedge.
He scampered to the bushes far away;
The shepherd called the ploughman to the fray;
The ploughman wished he had a gun to shoot.
The old dog barked and followed the pursuit.
The shepherd threw his hook and tottered past;
The ploughman ran but none could go so fast;
The woodman threw his faggot from the way
And ceased to chop and wondered at the fray.
But when he saw the dog and heard the cry
He threw his hatchet – but the fox was bye.
The shepherd broke his hook and lost the skin;
He found a badger hole and bolted in.
They tried to dig, but, safe from danger's way,
He lived to chase the hounds another day.

JOHN CLARE [1793–1864]

The
CREATION
— of —
FISHES

THE CREATION OF FISHES

from: Paradise Lost (Book VII)

Forthwith the Sounds and Seas, each Creek and Bay
With Frie innumerable swarme, and Shoales
Of Fish that with thir Finns and shining Scales
Glide under the green Wave, in Sculles that oft
Bank the mid Sea: part single or with mate
Graze the Sea weed thir pasture, and through Groves
Of Coral stray, or sporting with quick glance
Show to the Sun thir wav'd coats dropt with Gold,
Or in thir Pearlie shells at ease, attend
Moist nutriment, or under Rocks thir food
In jointed Armour watch: on smooth the Seale,
And bended Dolphins play: part huge of bulk
Wallowing unweildie, enormous in thir Gate
Tempest the Ocean: there Leviathan
Hugest of living Creatures, on the Deep
Stretcht like a Promontorie sleeps or swimmes,
And seems a moving Land, and at his Gilles
Draws in, and at his Trunck spouts out a Sea.

JOHN MILTON [1608–1674]

BALLADE TO A FISH OF THE BROOKE

Why flyest thou away with fear?
Trust me, there's nought of danger near,
  I have no wicked hooke
All covered with a snaring bait,
Alas, to tempt thee to thy fate,
  And dragge thee from the brooke.

O harmless tenant of the flood,
I do not wish to spill thy blood,
  For nature unto thee
Perchance hath given a tender wife,
And children dear, to charme thy life,
  As she hath done for me.

Enjoy thy streams, O harmless fish;
And when an angler, for his dish,
  Through gluttony's vile sin,
Attempts a wretch, to pull thee *out*,
God give thee strength, O gentel trout,
  To pull the raskall *in* !

JOHN WOLCOT [1738–1819]

FRESH-WATER FISH

from: Poly-Olbion

The Pearch with pricking finnes, against the Pike
  prepar'd,
As nature had thereon bestow'd this stronger guard,
His daintinesse to keepe, (each curious pallats
  proofe)
From his vile ravenous foe: next him I name the Ruffe,
His very neere ally, and both for scale and fin,
In taste, and for his bayte (indeed) his next of kin;
The pretty slender Dare, of many cald the Dace,
Within my liquid glasse, when Phœbus lookes his
  face,
Oft swiftly as he swimmes, his silver belly showes,
But with such nimble slight, that ere yee can disclose
His shape, out of your sight like lightning he is shot.
The Trout by Nature markt with many a crimson
  spot,
As though shee curious were in him above the rest,
And of fresh-water fish, did note him for the best;
The Roche, whose common kind to every flood doth
  fall;

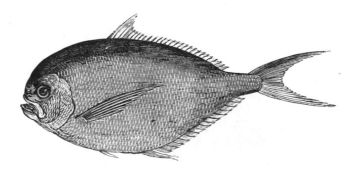

The Chub, (whose neater name) which some a Chevin
  call,
Food to the tyrant Pyke, (most being in his power)
Who for their numerous store he most doth them
  devoure;
The lustie Salmon then, from Neptunes watry realme,
When as his season serves, stemming my tydefull
  streame,
Then being in his kind, in me his pleasure takes,
(For whom the fisher than all other game forsakes)
Which bending of himselfe to th'fashion of a ring,
Above the forced weares, himselfe doth nimbly fling,
And often when the net hath dragd him safe to land,
Is seene by naturall force to scape his murderers hand:
Whose graine doth rise in flakes, with fatnesse inter-
  larded,
Of many a liquorish lip, that highly is regarded.
And Humber, to whose waste I pay my watry store,
Me of her Sturgeons sends, that I thereby the more
Should have my beauties grac'd, with some thing
  from him sent:
Not Ancums silvered Eele exceedeth that of Trent;
Though the sweet-smelling Smelt be more in Thames
  then me,

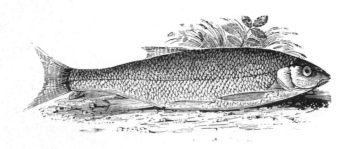

The Lamprey, and his lesse, in Severne generall be;
The Flounder smooth and flat, in other rivers caught,
Perhaps in greater store, yet better are not thought:
The daintie Gudgeon, Loche, the Minnow, and the
    Bleake,
Since they but little are, I little need to speake
Of them, nor doth it fit mee much of those to reck,
Which every where are found in every little beck;
Nor of the Crayfish here, which creepes amongst my
    stones,
From all the rest alone, whose shell is all his bones:
For Carpe, the Tench, and Breame, my other store
    among,
To lakes and standing pooles, that chiefly doe belong,
Here scowring in my foards, feed in my waters cleere,
Are muddy fish in ponds to that which they are heere.

MICHAEL DRAYTON [1563–1631]

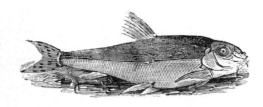

THE VOICE OF THE LOBSTER

'I passed by his garden, and marked, with one eye,
How the Owl and the Panther were sharing a pie:
The Panther took pie-crust, and gravy, and meat,
While the Owl had the dish as its share of the treat.
When the pie was all finished, the Owl, as a boon,
Was kindly permitted to pocket the spoon:
While the Panther received knife and fork with a growl,
And concluded the banquet by – '

''Tis the voice of the Lobster; I heard him declare,
"You have baked me too brown, I must sugar my hair."
As a duck with its eyelids, so he with his nose
Trims his belt and his buttons, and turns out his toes.
When the sands are all dry, he is gay as a lark,
And will talk in contemptuous tones of the Shark:
But, when the tide rises and sharks are around,
His voice has a timid and tremulous sound.'

LEWIS CARROLL [1832–1898]

THE CRAYFISH

I paid the fisherman on the sands,
And took the horrible brute in my hands,
A dubious being, a thing of the marge,
Hydra in small, wood-louse in large,
Formless as midnight, nameless as God.
It opened a gullet ugly and odd,
And tried to bite me; there came out
From its carapace a sort of snout;
God in the fearful order of Nature
Gave a dim place to the hideous creature;
It tried to bite me; we struggled hard;
It snapped my fingers – on their guard!
But the seller was scarcely out of sight
Behind a cliff, when it got its bite.
So I said, 'Live on and be blessed, poor beast,'
And cast it into the seething yeast,
Setting it free to depart and tell
To the murmuring ocean where it fell
The christening font of the rising sun,
That good, for ill, had once been done
By a human crab to a scaly one!

VICTOR HUGO [1802–1885]
(*Translated by* SIR GEORGE YOUNG)

THE MALDIVE SHARK

About the Shark, phlegmatical one,
Pale sot of the Maldive sea,
The sleek little pilot-fish, azure and slim,
How alert in attendance be.
From his saw-pit of mouth, from his charnel of maw,
They have nothing of harm to dread,
But liquidly glide on his ghastly flank
Or before his Gorgonian head;
Or lurk in the port of serrated teeth
In white triple tiers of glittering gates,
And there find a haven when peril's abroad,
An asylum in jaws of the Fates!
They are friends; and friendly they guide him to prey,
Yet never partake of the treat –
Eyes and brains to the dotard lethargic and dull,
Pale ravener of horrible meat.

HERMAN MELVILLE [1819–1891]

THE PIKE

From shadows of rich oaks outpeer
The moss-green bastions of the weir,
Where the quick dipper forages
In elver-peopled crevices.
And a small runlet trickling down the sluice
Gossamer music tries not to unloose.

Else round the broad pool's hush
    Nothing stirs.
Unless sometime a straggling heifer crush
Through the thronged spinny whence the pheasant whirs;
    Or martins in a flash
Come with wild mirth to dip their magical wings,
While in the shallow some doomed bulrush swings
    At whose hid root the diver vole's teeth gnash.

And nigh this toppling reed, still as the dead
    The great pike lies, the murderous patriarch,
    Watching the waterpit shelving and dark
Where through the plash his lithe bright vassals thread.

    The rose-finned roach and bluish bream
    And staring ruffe steal up the stream
    Hard by their glutted tyrant, now
    Still as a sunken bough.

    He on the sandbank lies,
        Sunning himself long hours
    With stony gorgon eyes:
        Westerward the hot sun lowers.

Sudden the gray pike changes, and quivering poises for
    slaughter;
  Intense terror wakens around him, the shoals scud awry, but
  there chances
  A chub unsuspecting; the prowling fins quicken, in fury he
  lances;
And the miller that opens the hatch stands amazed at the whirl
    in the water.

EDMUND BLUNDEN [1896–1974]

TO THE IMMORTAL MEMORY OF THE HALIBUT

ON WHICH I DINED THIS DAY

Where hast thou floated, in what seas pursued
Thy pastime? when wast thou an egg new-spawn'd,
Lost in th' immensity of ocean's waste?
Roar as they might, the overbearing winds
That rock'd the deep, thy cradle, thou wast safe –
And in thy minikin and embryo state,
Attach'd to the firm leaf of some salt weed,
Didst outlive tempests, such as wrung and rack'd
The joints of many a stout and gallant bark,
And whelm'd them in the unexplor'd abyss.
Indebted to no magnet and no chart,
Nor under guidance of the polar fire,
Thou wast a voyager on many coasts,
Grazing at large in meadows submarine,
Where flat Batavia just emerging peeps
Above the brine, – where Caledonia's rocks
Beat back the surge, – and where Hibernia shoots
Her wondrous causeway far into the main.
– Wherever thou hast fed, thou little thought'st,
And I not more, that I should feed on thee.
Peace therefore, and good health, and much good
    fish,
To him who sent thee! and success, as oft
As it descends into the billowy gulph,
To the same drag that caught thee! – Fare thee
    well!
Thy lot thy brethren of the slimy fin
Would envy, could they know that thou wast doom'd
To feed a bard, and to be prais'd in verse.

WILLIAM COWPER [1731–1800]

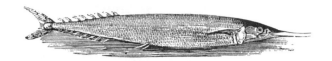

THE WORLD BELOW THE BRINE

The world below the brine,
Forests at the bottom of the sea, the branches and leaves,
Sea-lettuce, vast lichens, strange flowers and seeds, the thick
    tangle, openings, and pink turf,
Different colours, pale grey and green, purple, white, and gold,
    the play of light through the water,
Dumb swimmers there among the rocks, coral, gluten, grass,
    rushes, and the aliment of the swimmers,
Sluggish existences grazing there suspended, or slowly
    crawling close to the bottom,
The sperm-whale at the surface blowing air and spray, or
    disporting with his flukes,
The leaden-eyed shark, the walrus, the turtle, the hairy sea-
    leopard, and the sting-ray,
Passions there, wars, pursuits, tribes, sight in some ocean-
    depths, breathing that thick-breathing air, as so many
    do,
The change thence to the sight here, and to the subtle air
    breathed by beings like us who walk this sphere,
The change onward from ours to that of beings who walk
    other spheres.

WALT WHITMAN [1819–1892]

THE FISH

In a cool curving world he lies
And ripples with dark ecstasies.
The kind luxurious lapse and steal
Shapes all his universe to feel
And know and be; the clinging stream
Closes his memory, glooms his dream,
Who lips the roots o' the shore, and glides
Superb on unreturning tides.
Those silent waters weave for him
A fluctuant mutable world and dim,
Where wavering masses bulge and gape
Mysterious, and shape to shape
Dies momently through whorl and hollow,
And form and line and solid follow
Solid and line and form to dream
Fantastic down the eternal stream;
An obscure world, a shifting world,
Bulbous, or pulled to thin, or curled,
Or serpentine, or driving arrows,
Or serene slidings, or March narrows.

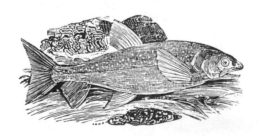

There slipping wave and shore are one,
And weed and mud. No ray of sun,
But glow to glow fades down the deep
(As dream to unknown dream in sleep);
Shaken translucency illumes
The hyaline of drifting glooms;
The strange soft-handed depth subdues
Drowned colour there, but black to hues,
As death to living, decomposes –
Red darkness of the heart of roses,
Blue brilliant from dead starless skies,
And gold that lies behind the eyes,
The unknown unnameable sightless white
That is the essential flame of night,
Lustreless purple, hooded green,
The myriad hues that lie between
Darkness and darkness!...
                  And all's one,
Gentle, embracing, quiet, dun,
The world he rests in, world he knows,
Perpetual curving. Only – grows
An eddy in that ordered falling,
A knowledge from the gloom, a calling
Weed in the wave, gleam in the mud –
The dark fire leaps along his blood;
Dateless and deathless, blind and still,
The intricate impulse works its will;
His woven world drops back; and he,
Sans providence, sans memory,
Unconscious and directly driven,
Fades to some dank sufficient heaven.
O world of lips, O world of laughter,

Where hope is fleet and thought flies after,
Of lights in the clear night, of cries
That drift along the wave and rise
Thin to the glittering stars above,
You know the hands, the eyes of love!
The strife of limbs, the sightless clinging,
The infinite distance, and the singing
Blown by the wind, a flame of sound,
The gleam, the flowers, and vast around
The horizon, and the heights above –
You know the sigh, the song of love!

But there the night is close, and there
Darkness is cold and strange and bare;
And the secret deeps are whisperless;
And rhythm is all deliciousness;
And joy is in the throbbing tide,
Whose intricate fingers beat and glide
In felt bewildering harmonies
Of trembling touch; and music is
The exquisite knocking of the blood.
Space is no more, under the mud;
His bliss is older than the sun.
Silent and straight the waters run.
The lights, the cries, the willows dim,
And the dark tide are one with him.

RUPERT BROOKE [1887–1915]

THE STURGEON

from: The Song of Hiawatha

On the white sand of the bottom
Lay the monster Mishe-Nahma,
Lay the sturgeon, King of Fishes;
Through his gills he breathed the water,
With his fins he fanned and winnowed,
With his tail he swept the sand-floor.
There he lay in all his armour;
On each side a shield to guard him,
Plates of bone upon his forehead,
Down his sides and back and shoulders
Plates of bone with spines projecting!
Painted was he with his war paints,
Strips of yellow, red, and azure,
Spots of brown and spots of sable;
And he lay there on the bottom,
Fanning with his fins of purple,
As above him Hiawatha
In his birch-canoe came sailing,
With his fishing-line of cedar.

HENRY WADSWORTH LONGFELLOW [1807–1882]

A JELLYFISH

Visible, invisible,
  a fluctuating charm
an amber-tinctured amethyst
  inhabits it, your arm
approaches and it opens
  and it closes; you had meant
to catch it and it quivers;
  you abandon your intent.

MARIANNE MOORE [1887–1972]

THE RAPE OF FISH

from: Progresse of the Soul

Is any kinde subject to rape like fish?
Ill unto man, they neither doe, nor wish:
Fishers they kill not, nor with noise awake,
They doe not hunt, nor strive to make a prey
Of beasts, nor their yong sonnes to beare away;
Foules they pursue not, nor do undertake
To spoile the nests industrious birds do make;
Yet them all these unkinde kinds feed upon,
To kill them is an occupation,
  And lawes make Fasts, and Lents for their destruction.

JOHN DONNE [1573–1631]

170

THE SALMON

from: Poly-Olbion

And when the Salmon seeks a fresher stream to find,
Which hither from the sea comes yearly by his kind;
As he towards season grows, and stems the wat'ry tract
Where Tivy, falling down, makes an high cataract,
Forced by the rising rocks that there her course oppose,
As though within her bounds they meant her to enclose, –
Here, when the laboring fish does at the foot arrive,
And finds that by his strength he does but vainly strive;
His tail takes in his mouth, and, bending like a bow
That's to full compass drawn, aloft himself doth throw,
Then springing at his height, as doth a little wand,
That, bended end to end, and started from man's hand,
Far off itself doth cast; so does the Salmon vault:
And if at first he fail, his second summersault
He instantly essays; and, from his nimble ring
Still yerking, never leaves until himself he fling
Above the opposing stream.

MICHAEL DRAYTON [1563–1631]

SHELL-FISH

from: Poly-Olbion

Amongst whose sundry sorts, since thus farre I am in,
Ile of our shell-fish speake, with these of scale and fin:
   The sperme-increasing Crab, much cooking that
     doth aske,
The big-legg'd Lobster, fit for wanton Venus taske,
Voluptuaries oft take rather then for food,
And that the same effect which worketh in the blood
The rough long Oyster is, much like the Lobster
     limb'd:
The Oyster hote as they, the Mussle often trimd
With orient pearle within, as thereby Nature show'd,
That she some secret good had on that shell bestow'd:
The Scallop cordiall judged, the dainty Wilk and Limp,
The Periwincle, Prawne, the Cockle, and the
     Shrimpe,
For wanton womens tasts, or for weake stomacks
     bought.

MICHAEL DRAYTON [1563–1631]

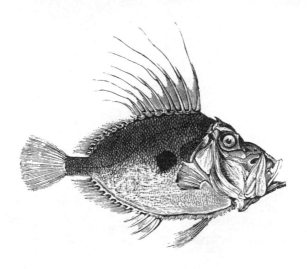

SOME SALT-WATER FISH

from: Poly-Olbion

What fish can any shore, or British sea-towne show,
That's eatable to us, that it doth not bestow
Abundantly thereon? the Herring King of sea,
The faster feeding Cod, the Mackrell brought by
    May,
The daintie Sole, and Plaice, the Dabb, as of their
    blood;
The Conger finely sous'd, hote summers coolest food;
The Whiting knowne to all a generall wholesome
    dish;
The Gurnet, Rochet, Mayd, and Mullet, dainty fish;
The Haddock, Turbet, Bert, fish nourishing and
    strong;

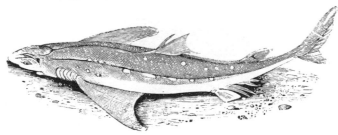

The Thornback, and the Scate, provocative among:
The Weaver, which although his prickles venom bee,
By fishers cut away, which buyers seldome see:
Yet for the fish he beares, tis not accounted bad;
The Sea-Flounder is here as common as the Shad;
The Sturgeon cut to Keggs, (too big to handle whole)
Gives many a dainty bit out of his lusty jole.
Yet of rich Neptunes store, whilst thus I idely chat,
Thinke not that all betwixt the Wherpoole, and the
    Sprat,
I goe about to name, that were to take in hand,
The atomy to tell, or to cast up the sand;
But on the English coast, those most that usuall are,
Wherewith the staules from thence doe furnish us for
    farre.

MICHAEL DRAYTON [1563–1631]

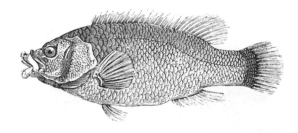

174

THE SHARK

A treacherous monster is the Shark,
He never makes the least remark.

And when he sees you on the sand,
He doesn't seem to want to land.

He watches you take off your clothes,
And not the least excitement shows.

His eyes do not grow bright or roll,
He has astounding self-control.

He waits till you are quite undrest,
And seems to take no interest.

And when towards the sea you leap,
He looks as if he were asleep.

But when you once get in his range,
His whole demeanour seems to change.

He throws his body right about,
And his true character comes out.

It's no use crying or appealing,
He seems to lose all decent feeling.

After this warning you will wish
To keep clear of this treacherous fish.

His back is black, his stomach white,
He has a very dangerous bite.

LORD ALFRED DOUGLAS [1870–1945]

THE FISHES AND THE CORMORANT

No pond nor pool within his haunt
But paid a certain cormorant
Its contribution from its fishes,
And stock'd his kitchen with good dishes.
  Yet, when old age the bird had chill'd,
  His kitchen was less amply fill'd.
  All cormorants, however grey,
  Must die, or for themselves purvey.
  But ours had now become so blind,
  His finny prey he could not find;
  And, having neither hook nor net,
  His appetite was poorly met.
What hope, with famine thus infested?
  Necessity, whom history mentions,
  A famous mother of inventions,
The following stratagem suggested:
  He found upon the water's brink
  A crab, to which said he, 'My friend,
  A weighty errand let me send:
    Go quicker than a wink –
    Down to the fishes sink,
  And tell them they are doom'd to die;
  For, ere eight days have hasten'd by,
  Its lord will fish this water dry.'
The crab, as fast as she could scrabble,
Went down, and told the scaly rabble.
What bustling, gathering, agitation!
Straight up they send a deputation
  To wait upon the ancient bird.
  'Sir Cormorant, whence hast thou heard
    This dreadful news? And what
  Assurance of it has thou got?
  How such a danger can we shun?

Prey tell us, what is to be done?'
'Why, change your dwelling-place,' said he,
'What, change our dwelling! How can we?'
'O, by your leave, I'll take that care,
And, one by one, in safety bear
    You all to my retreat:
        The path's unknown
         To any feet,
       Except my own.
A pool, scoop'd out by Nature's hands,
Amidst the desert rocks and sands,
Where human traitors never come,
Shall save your people from their doom.'
The fish republic swallow'd all,
And, coming at the fellow's call,
Were singly borne away to stock
A pond beneath a lonely rock;
And there good prophet cormorant,
  Proprietor and bailiff sole,
  From narrow water, clear and shoal,
With ease supplied his daily want,
And taught them, at their own expense,

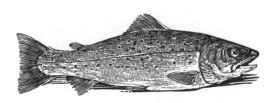

That heads well stored with common sense
Give no devourers confidence. –
Still did the change not hurt their case,
Since, had they staid, the human race,
Successful by pernicious art,
Would have consumed as large a part.
What matters who your flesh devours,
Of human or of bestial powers?
In this respect, or wild or tame,
All stomachs seem to me the same:
The odds is small, in point of sorrow,
Of death to-day, or death to-morrow.

JEAN DE LA FONTAINE [1621–1695]
(*Translated by* ELIZUR WRIGHT)

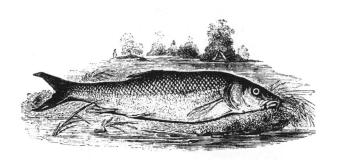

GOLD AND SILVER FISHES IN A POOL

from: Yarrow Revisited

While musing here I sit in shadow cool,
And watch these mute Companions in the pool,
(Among reflected boughs of leafy trees)
By glimpses caught – disporting at their ease –
Enlivened, braced, by hardy luxuries,
I ask what warrant fixed them (like a spell
Of witchcraft, fixed them) in the crystal cell;
To wheel, with languid motion, round and round
Beautiful, yet in mournful durance bound.
Their peace, perhaps, our lightest footfall marred,
On their quick sense our sweetest music jarred;
And whither could they dart, if seized with fear?
No sheltering stone, no tangled root was near.
When fire or taper ceased to cheer the room,
They wore away the night in starless gloom;
And when the sun first dawned upon the streams,
How faint their portion of his vital beams!
Thus, and unable to complain, they fared,
While not one joy of ours by them was shared.

WILLIAM WORDSWORTH [1770–1850]

THE FISH AND THE MAN

You strange, astonished-looking, angle-faced,
  Dreary-mouthed, gaping wretches of the sea,
  Gulping salt-water everlastingly,
Cold-blooded, though with red your blood be graced,
And mute, though dwellers in the roaring waste;
  And you, all shapes beside, that fishy be, –
  Some round, some flat, some long, all devilry,
Legless, unloving, infamously chaste: –

O scaly, slippery, wet swift, staring wights,
  What is't ye do? What life lead? eh, dull goggles?
How do ye vary your vile days and nights?
  How pass your Sundays? Are ye still but joggles
In ceaseless wash? Still nought but gapes, and bites,
  And drinks, and stares, diversified with boggles?

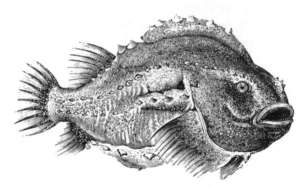

A FISH ANSWERS
Amazing monster! that, for aught I know,
  With the first sight of thee didst make our race
  For ever stare! O flat and shocking face,
Grimly divided from the breast below!
Thou that on dry land horribly dost go
  With a split body and most ridiculous pace,

180

Prong after prong, disgracer of all grace,
Long-useless-finned, haired, upright, unwet, slow!

O breather of unbreathable, sword-sharp air,
　　How canst exist? How bear thyself, thou dry
And dreary sloth? What particle canst share
　　Of the only blessed life, the watery?
I sometimes see of ye an actual *pair*
　　Go by! linked fin by fin! most odiously.

LEIGH HUNT [1784–1859]

TROUT STREAM

from: The Brook

I wind about, and in and out,
　　With here a blossom sailing,
And here and there a lusty trout,
　　And here and there a grayling.

And here and there a foamy flake
　　Upon me, as I travel
With many a silvery waterbreak
　　Above the golden gravel,

And draw them all along, and flow
　　To join the brimming river,
For men may come and men may go,
　　But I go on for ever.

LORD TENNYSON [1809–1892]

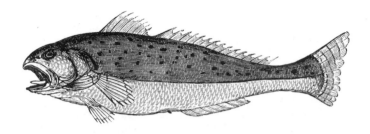

REJOICE IN FISH

from: Jubilate Agno

Let James rejoice with the Skuttle-Fish, who foils his
  foe by the effusion of his ink.
Let John rejoice with Nautilus who spreads his sail &
  plies his oar, and the Lord is his pilot.
Let Philip rejoice with Boca, which is a fish that can
  speak.
Let Bartholemew rejoice with the Eel, who is pure in
  proportion to where he is found & how he is used.
Let Thomas rejoice with the Sword-Fish, whose aim
  is perpetual & strength insuperable.
Let Matthew rejoice with Uranoscopus, whose eyes
  are lifted up to God.
Let James the less, rejoice with the Haddock, who
  brought the piece of money for the Lord and Peter.
Let Jude bless with the Bream, who is of melancholy
  from his depth and serenity.

Let Simon rejoice with the Sprat, who is pure and
innumerable.
Let Matthias rejoice with the Flying-Fish, who has a
part with the birds, and is sublimity in his conceit.
Let Stephen rejoice with Remora – The Lord remove
all obstacles to his glory.
Let Paul rejoice with the Seale, who is pleasant &
faithfull, like God's good ENGLISHMAN.
Let Agrippa, which is Agricola, rejoice with Elops,
who is a choice fish.
Let Joseph rejoice with the Turbut, whose capture
makes the poor fisher-man sing.
Let John, the Baptist, rejoice with the Salmon –
blessed be the name of the Lord Jesus for infant
Baptism.
Let Mark rejoice with the Mullet, who is John Dore,
God be gracious to him & his family.
Let Barnabas rejoice with the Herring – God be
gracious to the Lord's fishery.
Let Cleopas rejoice with the Mackerel, who cometh
in a shoal after a leader.
Let Abiud of the Lord's line rejoice with Murex, who
is good and of a precious tincture.

Let Eliakim rejoice with the Shad, who is contemned
in his abundance.
Let Azor rejoice with the Flounder, who is both of
the sea and of the river.
Let Sadoc rejoice with the Bleak, who playeth upon
the surface in the Sun.
Let Achim rejoice with the Miller's Thumb, who is a
delicious morsel for the waterfowl.
Let Eliud rejoice with Cinædus, who is a fish yellow
all over.
Let Eleazar rejoice with the Grampus, who is a
pompous spouter.

CHRISTOPHER SMART [1722–1771]

A FISH RIDDLE

Although it's cold no clothes I wear,
Frost and snow I do not fear,
I have no use for hose or shoes
Although I travel far and near.
All I eat comes free to me,
I need no cider, ale or sack,
I nothing buy or sell or lack.

ANONYMOUS

(*Answer: A herring in the sea*)

The
CREATION
— of —
INSECTS

THE CREATION OF INSECTS

from: Paradise Lost (Book VII)

                          First crept
The Parsimonious Emmet, provident
Of future, in small room large heart enclos'd,
Pattern of just equalitie perhaps
Hereafter, join'd in her popular Tribes
Of Commonaltie: swarming next appeer'd
The Female Bee that feeds her Husband Drone
Deliciously, and builds her waxen Cells
With Honey stor'd: the rest are numberless,
And thou thir Natures know'st, and gav'st them Names....

JOHN MILTON [1608–1674]

INSECTS

These tiny loiterers on the barley's beard,
And happy units of a numerous herd
Of playfellows, the laughing Summer brings,
Mocking the sunshine in their glittering wings,
How merrily they creep, and run, and fly!
No kin they bear to labour's drudgery,
Smoothing the velvet of the pale hedge-rose;
And where they fly for dinner no one knows –
The dew-drops feed them not – they love the shine
Of noon, whose sun may bring them golden wine.
All day they're playing in their Sunday dress –
Till night goes sleep, and they can do no less;
Then, to the heath bell's silken hood they fly,
And like to princes in their slumbers lie,
Secure from night, and dropping dews, and all,
In silken beds and roomy painted hall.
So merrily they spend their summer day,
Now in the cornfields, now the new-mown hay.
One almost fancies that such happy things,
With coloured hoods and richly burnished wings,
And fairy folk, in splendid masquerade
Disguised, as if of mortal folk afraid,
Keeping their merry pranks a mystery still,
Lest glaring day should do their secrets ill.

JOHN CLARE [1793–1864]

THE GLOWORME

Stay, fairest Chariessa, stay and mark
This animated Gem, whose fainter spark
Of fading light, its birth had from the dark:

A Star thought by the erring Passenger,
Which falling from its native Orb dropt here,
And makes the Earth (its Centre), now its Sphere.

Should many of these sparks together be,
He that the unknown light far off should see,
Would think it a terrestrial Galaxie.

Take't up, fair Saint; see how it mocks thy fright,
The paler flame doth not yield heat, though light,
Which thus deceives thy Reason, through thy sight.

But see how quickly it (ta'ne up) doth fade,
To shine in darkness onely being made,
By th' brightness of thy light turn'd to a shade;

And burnt to ashes by thy flaming eyes
On the chaste Altar of thy hand it dies,
As to thy greater light a sacrifice.

THOMAS STANLEY [1625–1678]

HONY BEES

from: Henry V

... for so worke the Hony Bees,
Creatures that by a rule in Nature teach
The Act of Order to a peopled Kingdome.
They have a King, and Officers of sorts;
Where some like Magistrates correct at home,
Others, like Merchants venter Trade abroad:
Others, like Souldiers armed in their stings,
Make boote upon the Summer's Velvet buddes:
Which pillage, they with merry march bring home
To the Tent-royal of their Emperor:
Who busied in his Majesty surveyes
The singing Masons building roofes of Gold,
The civil Citizens kneading up the hony;
The poore Mechanicke Porters, crowding in
Their heavy burthens at his narrow gate:
The sad-ey'd Justice with his surly humme,
Delivering ore to Executors pale
The lazie yawning Drone.

WILLIAM SHAKESPEARE [1564–1616]

THE SPIDER AND THE FLY

'Will you walk into my parlour?' said the Spider to the Fly, –
'’Tis the prettiest little parlour that ever you did spy;
The way into my parlour is up a winding stair,
And I have many curious things to show when you are there.'
'Oh no, no,' said the little Fly, 'to ask me is in vain,
For who goes up your winding stair can ne'er come down again.'

'I'm sure you must be weary, dear, with soaring up so high;
Will you rest upon my little bed?' said the Spider to the Fly.
'There are pretty curtains drawn around, the sheets are fine
    and thin,
And if you like to rest a while, I'll snugly tuck you in!'
'Oh no, no,' said the little Fly, 'for I've often heard it said,
They never, never wake again, who sleep upon your bed!'

Said the cunning Spider to the Fly: 'Dear friend, what can I do
To prove the warm affection I've always felt for you?
I have, within my pantry, good store of all that's nice;
I'm sure you're very welcome – will you please to take a slice?'
'Oh no, no,' said the little Fly, 'kind sir, that cannot be,
I've heard what's in your pantry, and I do not wish to see!'

'Sweet creature,' said the Spider, 'you're witty and you're
    wise;
How handsome are your gauzy wings, how brilliant are your
    eyes!
I have a little looking-glass upon my parlour shelf,
If you'll step in one moment, dear, you shall behold yourself.'
'I thank you, gentle sir,' she said, 'for what you're pleased
    to say,
And bidding you good-morning now, I'll call another day.'

The Spider turned him round about, and went into his den,
For well he knew the silly Fly would soon come back again;
So he wove a subtle web, in a little corner sly,
And set his table ready, to dine upon the Fly.
Then he came out to his door again, and merrily did sing, –
'Come hither, hither, pretty Fly, with the pearl and silver
    wing;
Your robes are green and purple, there's a crest upon your head;
Your eyes are like the diamond bright, but mine are dull as
    lead!'

Alas, alas! how very soon this silly little Fly,
Hearing his wily, flattering words, came slowly flitting by:
With buzzing wings she hung aloft, then near and nearer drew, –
Thinking only of her brilliant eyes, and green and purple hue,
Thinking only of her crested head – poor foolish thing! At last
Up jumped the cunning Spider, and fiercely held her fast;
He dragged her up his winding stair, into his dismal den,
Within his little parlour – but she ne'er came out again!

MARY HOWITT [1799–1888]

THE WASP

Once as I went by rail to Epping Street,
Both windows being open, a wasp flew in;
Through the compartment swung and almost out
Scarce seen, scarce heard; but dead against the pane
Entitled 'Smoking', did the train's career
Arrest her passage. Such a wonderful
Impervious transparency, before
That palpitating moment, had never yet
Her airy voyage thwarted. Undismayed,
With diligence incomparable, she sought
An exit, till the letters like a snare
Entangled her; or else the frosted glass
And signature indelible appeared
The key to all the mystery: there she groped,
And flirted petulant wings, and fiercely sang
A counter-spell against the sorcery,
The sheer enchantment that inhibited
Her access to the world – her birthright there!
So visible, and so beyond her reach!
Baffled and raging like a tragic queen,
She left at last the stencilled tablet; roamed
The pane a while to cool her regal ire,
Then tentatively touched the window-frame:
Sure footing still, though rougher than the glass;
Dissimilar in texture, and so obscure!

Perplexed now by opacity with foot and wing
She coasted up and down the wood and worked
Her wrath to passion-point again. Then from the frame
She slipped by chance into the open space
Left by the lowered sash: – the world once more
In sight! She paused; she closed her wings, and left
The air with learned antennæ for the smooth
Resistance that she knew now must belong
To such mysterious transparences.
No foothold? Down she fell – six inches down! –
Hovered a second, dazed and dubious still;
Then soared away a captive queen set free.

JOHN DAVIDSON [1857–1900]

TO A LOUSE

On seeing one on a lady's bonnet at church

Ha! whare ye gaun, ye crowling ferlie!
Your impudence protects you sairlie:
I canna say but ye strunt rarely,
    Owre gauze and lace;
Tho' faith, I fear, ye dine but sparely
    On sic a place.

Ye ugly, creepin, blastit wonner,
Detested, shunn'd, by saunt and sinner,
How daur ye set your fit upon her,
    Sae fine a Lady!
Gae somewhere else and seek your dinner,
    On some poor body.

Swith, in some beggar's haffet squattle;
There ye may creep, and sprawl, and sprattle
Wi' ither kindred, jumping cattle,
    In shoals and nations;
Whare horn nor bane de'er daur unsettle
    Your thick plantations.

Now haud you there, ye're out o' sight,
Below the fatt'rels, snug and tight;
Na faith ye yet! ye'll no be right
    Till ye've got on it,
The vera tapmost, tow'ring height
    O' Miss's bonnet.

My sooth! right bauld ye set your nose out,
As plump an' gray as onie grozet:
O for some rank, mercurial rozet,
      Or fell, red smeddum,
I'd gie ye sic a hearty dose o't,
      Wad dress your doddum!

I wad na been surpris'd to spy
On an auld wife's flainen toy;
Or aiblins some bit duddie boy,
      On's wyliecoat;
But Miss's fine Lunardi! fye!
      How daur ye do't?

O Jenny, dinna toss your head,
And set your beauties a' abread!
Ye little ken what cursed speed
      The blastie's makin!
Thae winks and finger-ends, I dread,
      Are notice takin!

O wad some Pow'r the giftie gie us
To see oursels as others see us!
It wad frae monie a blunder free us
      An' foolish notion:
What airs in dress an' gait wad lea'e us,
      An' ev'n Devotion.

ROBERT BURNS [1759–1796]

THE STUDY OF A SPIDER

From holy flower to holy flower
Thou weavest thine unhallowed bower.
The harmless dewdrops, beaded thin,
Ripple along thy ropes of sin.
Thy house a grave, a gulf thy throne
Affright the fairies every one.
Thy winding sheets are grey and fell,
Imprisoning with nets of hell
The lovely births that winnow by,
Winged sisters of the rainbow sky:
Elf-darlings, fluffy, bee-bright things
And owl-white moths with mealy wings,
And tiny flies, as gauzy thin
As e'er were shut electrum in.
These are thy death spoils, insect ghoul,
With their dear life thy fangs are foul.
Thou felon anchorite of pain
Who sittest in a world of slain.
Hermit, who tunest song unsweet
To heaving wing and writhing feet.
A glutton of creation's sighs,
Miser of many miseries.
Toper, whose lonely feasting chair
Sways in inhospitable air.
The board is bare, the bloated host
Drinks to himself toast after toast.
His lip requires no goblet brink,
But like a weasel must he drink.
The vintage is as old as time
And bright as sunset, pressed and prime.

Ah, venom mouth and shaggy thighs
And paunch grown sleek with sacrifice,
Thy dolphin back and shoulders round

Coarse-hairy, as some goblin hound
Whom a hag rides to sabbath on,
While shuddering stars in fear grown wan.
Thou palace priest of treachery,
Thou type of selfish lechery,
I break the toils around thy head
And from their gibbets take thy dead.

LORD DE TABLEY [1835–1895]

THE VILLAIN SPIDER

from: The Seasons

But chief to heedless flies the window proves
A constant death; where, gloomily retir'd,
The villain spider lives, cunning and fierce, –
Mixture abhorr'd! Amid a mangled heap
Of carcasses, in eager watch he sits,
O'erlooking all his waving snares around.
Near the dire cell the dreadless wanderer oft
Passes, as oft the ruffian shows his front;
The prey at last ensnar'd, he dreadful darts,
With rapid glide, along the leaning line;
And, fixing in the wretch his cruel fangs,
Strikes backward grimly pleased: the fluttering wing
And shriller sound declare extreme distress,
And ask the helping hospitable hand.

JAMES THOMSON [1700–1748]

ON FINDING A SMALL FLY
CRUSHED IN A BOOK

Some hand, that never meant to do thee hurt,
Has crush'd thee here between these pages pent;
But thou has left thine own fair monument,
Thy wings gleam out and tell me what thou wert:
Oh! that the memories, which survive us here,
Were half as lovely as these wings of thine!
Pure relics of a blameless life, that shine
Now thou art gone: Our doom is ever near:
The peril is beside us day by day;
The book will close upon us, it may be,
Just as we lift ourselves to soar away
Upon the summer-airs.   But, unlike thee,
The closing book may stop our vital breath,
Yet leave no lustre on our page of death.

CHARLES TENNYSON TURNER [1808–1879]

FLEAS

from: On Poetry

So, naturalists observe, a flea
Hath smaller fleas that on him prey;
And these have smaller fleas to bite 'em,
And so proceed *ad infinitum.*

JONATHAN SWIFT [1667–1745]

IN PRAISE OF INSECTS

from: Jubilate Agno

Let Elthan praise with the Flea, his coat of mail, his
    piercer, and his vigour, which wisdom and provi-
    dence have contrived to attract observation and to
    escape it.
Let Heman bless with the Spider, his warp and his
    woof, his sublety and industry, which are good.
Let Chalcol praise with the Beetle, whose life is
    precious in the sight of God, tho' his appearance is
    against him.
Let Huldah bless with the Silkworm – the orna-
    ments of the Proud are from the bowells of their
    Betters.
Let Susanna bless with the Butterfly – beauty hath
    wings, but chastity is the Cherub.
Let Sampson bless with the Bee, to whom the Lord
    hath given strength to annoy the assailant and wis-
    dom to his strength.
Let Amasiah bless with the Chaffer – the top of tree is
    for the brow of the champion, who has given the
    glory to God.
Let Hashum bless with the Fly, whose health is the
    honey of the air, but he feeds upon the thing
    strangled, and perisheth.

CHRISTOPHER SMART [1722–1771]

A FLY CAUGHT IN A COBWEB

Small type of great ones, that do hum
Within this whole world's narrow room,
That with a busie hollow noise
Catch at the people's vainer voice,
And with spread sails play with their breath,
Whose very hails new christen death.
Poor Fly, caught in an airy net,
Thy wings have fetter'd now thy feet;
Where, like a Lyon in a toyl,
Howere thou keep'st a noble coyl,
And beat'st thy gen'rous breast, that o're
The plains thy fatal buzzes rore,
Till thy all-bellyd foe (round elf)
Hath quarter'd thee within himself.

   Was it not better once to play
I' th' light of a majestick ray,
Where, though too neer and bold, the fire
Might sindge thy upper down attire,
And thou i' th' storm to loose an eye,
A wing, or a self-trapping thigh:
Yet hadst thou fal'n like him, whose coil
Made fishes in the sea to broyl,
When now th'ast scap'd the noble flame;
Trapp'd basely in a slimy frame,
And free of air, thou art become
Slave to the sprawn of mud and lome?

Nor is't enough thy self do's dresse
To thy swoln lord a num'rous messe,
And by degrees thy thin veins bleed,
And piecemeal dost his poyson feed;
But now devour'd, art like to be
A net spun for thy familie,
And, straight expanded in the air,
Hang'st for thy issue too a snare.
Strange witty death and cruel ill
That, killing thee, thou thine dost kill!
Like pies, in whose entombed ark
All fowl crowd downward to a lark,
Thou art thine en'mies' sepulcher,
And in thee buriest, too, thine heir.

Yet Fates a glory have reserv'd
For one so highly hath deserv'd.
As the rhinoceros doth dy
Under his castle-enemy,
As through the cranes trunk throat doth speed,
The aspe doth on his feeder feed;
Fall yet triumphant in thy woe,
Bound with the entrails of thy foe.

RICHARD LOVELACE [1618–1658]

AN AUGUST MIDNIGHT

A shaded lamp and a waving blind,
And the beat of a clock from a distant floor:
On this scene enter – winged, horned, and spined –
A longlegs, a moth, and a dumbledore;
While 'mid my page there idly stands
A sleepy fly, that rubs its hands ...

Thus meet we five in this still place
At this point of time, at this point in space.
– My guests besmear my new-penned line,
Or bang at the lamp and fall supine.
'God's humblest, they!' I muse. Yet why?
They know earth-secrets that know not I.

THOMAS HARDY [1840–1928]

206

TO THE GRASSHOPPER AND THE CRICKET

Green little vaulter in the sunny grass,
Catching your heart up at the feel of June,
Sole voice that's heard amidst the lazy noon,
When even the bees lag at the summoning brass:
And you, warm little housekeeper, who class
With those who think the candles come too soon,
Loving the fire, and with your tricksome tune
Nick the glad silent moments as they pass:
Oh, sweet and tiny cousins, that belong
One to the fields, the other to the hearth,
Both have your sunshine; both, though small, are
     strong
At your clear hearts; and both seem given to earth
To ring in thoughtful ears this natural song –
Indoors and out, summer and winter – mirth.

LEIGH HUNT [1784–1859]

THE GRASSHOPPER

Oh thou that swing'st upon the waving hair
   Of some well-filled oaten beard,
Drunk ev'ry night with a delicious tear
   Dropp'd thee from Heav'n, where now th' art rear'd.

The joys of earth and air are thine entire,
   That with thy feet and wings dost hop and fly;
And when thy poppy works thou dost retire
   To thy carv'd acron bed to lie.

Up with the day, the sun thou welcom'st then,
   Sport'st in the gilt plaits of his beams,
And all these merry days mak'st merry men,
   Thyself, and melancholy streams.

But ah the sickle! Golden ears are cropp'd;
   Ceres and Bacchus bid goodnight;
Sharp frosty fingers all your flow'rs have topp'd,
   And what scythes spar'd, winds shave off quite.

Poor verdant fool! And now green ice! Thy joys
   Large and as lasting as thy perch of grass,
Bid us lay in 'gainst winter rain, and poise
   Their floods with an o'erflowing glass.

Thou best of men and friends! We will create
    A genuine Summer in each other's breast;
And, spite of this cold time and frozen fate,
    Thaw us a warm seat to our rest.

Our sacred hearths shall burn eternally
    As vestal flames; the North-wind, he
Shall strike his frost-stretch'd wings, dissolved and
      fly,
    This Etna in epitome.

Dropping December shall come weeping in,
    Bewail th'usurping of his reign;
But when in show'rs of old Greek we begin,
    Shall cry, He hath his crown again!

Night as clear Hesper shall our tapers whip
    From the light casements where we play,
And the dark hag from her black mantle strip,
    And stick there everlasting day.

Thus richer than untempted kings are we,
    That asking nothing, nothing need:
Though lord of all what seas embrace, yet he
    That wants himself, is poor indeed.

RICHARD LOVELACE [1618–1658]

THE POET AND THE FLY

Round the Poet, ere he slumbered,
Sang the Fly thro' hours unnumbered;
Sauntered, if he seemed to doze,
O'er the arch that was his nose,
Darting thence to re-appear
In his subtly-chambered ear:
When at last he slept right soundly,
It transfixed him so profoundly,
Caused him agony so horrid,
That he woke and smote his forehead
(It's the course that poets take
When they're trifled with) and spake: –

'Fly! Thy brisk unmeaning buzz
Would have roused the man of Uz;
And, besides thy buzzing, I
Fancy thou'rt a stinging fly.
Fly – who'rt peering, I am certain,
At me now from yonder curtain:
Busy, curious, thirsty fly
(As thou'rt clept, I well know why) –
Cease, if only for a single
Hour, to make my being tingle!
Flee to some loved haunt of thine;
To the valleys where the kine,
Udder-deep in grasses cool,
Or the rushy-margined pool,
Strive to lash thy murmurous kin
(Vainly) from their dappled skin!
Round the steed's broad nostrils flit,
Till he foams and champs the bit,
And, reluctant to be bled,
Tosses high his lordly head.

I have seen a thing no larger
Than thyself assail a charger;
He – who unconcerned would stand
All the braying of the band,
Who disdained trombone and drum –
Quailed before that little hum.
I have seen one flaunt his feelers
'Fore the steadiest of wheelers,
And at once the beast would bound,
Kangaroo-like, off the ground.
Lithe o'er moor and marish hie,
Like thy king, the Dragon-Fly;
With the burnished bee skim over
Sunlit uplands white with clover;
Or, low-brooding on the lea,
Warn the swain of storms to be!
– Need I tell thee how to act?
Do just anything in fact.
Haunt my cream ('twill make thee plump),
Filch my sugar, every lump;
Round my matin-coat keep dodging,
In my necktie find a lodging
(Only, now that I reflect, I
Rather seldom wear a necktie);
Perforate my Sunday hat;
(It's a new one – what of that?)
Honeycomb my cheese, my favourite,
Thy researches will but flavour it;
Spoil my dinner-beer, and sneak up
Basely to my evening tea-cup;
Palter with my final toddy;
But respect my face and body!
Hadst thou been a painted hornet,

Or a wasp, I might have borne it;
But a common fly or gnat!
Come, my friend, get out of that.'

Dancing down, the insect here
Stung him smartly on the ear;
For a while – like some cheap earring –
Clung there, then retreated jeering.
(As men jeer, in prose or rhyme,
So may flies, in pantomime;
We discern not in their buzz
Language, but the poet does.)

Long he deemed him at Death's door;
Then sprang featly to the floor,
Seized his water-jug and drank its
Whole contents; hung several blankets
Round his lair and pinned them fast:
'I shall rest,' he moaned, 'at last.'
But anon a ghastlier groan
To the shuddering night made known
That with blanket and with pin
He had shut the creature IN.

C. S. CALVERLEY [1831–1884]

THE FLY

Little Fly,
Thy summer's play
My thoughtless hand
Has brush'd away.

Am not I
A fly like thee?
Or art not thou
A man like me?

For I dance,
And drink, & sing,
Till some blind hand
Shall brush my wing.

If thought is life
And strength & breath,
And the want
Of thought is death;

Then am I
A happy fly,
If I live
Or if I die.

WILLIAM BLAKE [1757–1827]

LITTLE ANT

from: The Ant

Forbear, thou great good husband, little ant;
  A little respite from thy flood of sweat!
Thou, thine own horse and cart under this plant,
  Thy spacious tent, fan thy prodigious heat;
Down with thy double load of that one grain!
It is a granary for all thy train.

Austere and cynick! not one hour t' allow,
  To lose with pleasure, what thou got'st with pain;
But drive on sacred festivals thy plow,
  Tearing high-ways with thy ore-chargëd wain,
Not all thy life-time one poor minute live,
And thy ore-labour'd bulk with mirth relieve?

Thus we unthrifty thrive within earth's tomb
  For some more rav'nous and ambitious jaw:
The grain in th' ant's, the ant in the pie's womb,
  The pie in th' hawk's, the hawk ith' eagle's maw.
So scattering to hoard 'gainst a long day,
Thinking to save all, we cast all away.

RICHARD LOVELACE [1618–1658]

LINES TO A DRAGON-FLY

Life (priest and poet say) is but a dream;
 I wish no happier one than to be laid
 Beneath a cool syringa's scented shade,
Or wavy willow, by the running stream,
 Brimful of moral, where the dragon-fly,
 Wanders as careless and content as I.
Thanks for this fancy, insect king,
Of purple crest and filmy wing,
Who with indifference givest up
The water-lily's golden cup,
To come again and overlook
What I am writing in my book.
Believe me, most who read the line
Will read with hornier eyes than thine;
And yet their souls shall live for ever,
And thine drop dead into the river!
God pardon them, O insect king,
Who fancy so unjust a thing!

WALTER SAVAGE LANDOR [1775–1864]

THE GNAT

One Night all tired with the weary Day,
And with my tedious selfe, I went to lay
    My fruitlesse Cares
    And needlesse feares
      Asleep.

The curtaines of the Bed, and of mine Eyes
Being drawne, I hop'd no trouble would surprise
    That Rest which now
    'Gan on my Brow
      To creep.

When loe a little flie, lesse than its Name
(It was a Gnat) with angry Murmur came.
    About She flew
    And louder grew
      Whilst I
Faine would have scorn'd the silly Thing, and slept
Out all its Noise; I resolute silence kept,
    And laboured so
    To overthrow
      The Flie.

But still with sharp Alarms vexatious She
Or challenged, or rather mocked Me.
    Angry at last
    About I cast
      My Hand.
'Twas well Night would not let me blush, nor see
With whom I fought; And yet though feeble She
    Nor Her nor my
    Owne Wrath could I
      Command.

Away She flies, and Her owne Triumph sings
I being left to fight with idler Things,
    A feeble pair
    My Selfe and Aire.
        How true
A worme is Man, whom flies their sport can make!
Poor worme; true Rest in no Bed can he take,
    But one of Earth
    Whence He came forth
        And grew.

For there None but his silent Sisters be,
Wormes of as true and genuine Earth as He,
    Which from the same
    Corruption came:
        And there
Though on his Eyes they feed, though on his Heart,
They neither vex nor wake Him; every part
    Rests in sound sleep,
    And out doth keep
        All feare.

JOSEPH BEAUMONT [1616–1699]

THE CRICKET

Where art thou, merry whistler of the hearth?
What time the grate is stuffed with arid moss,
I miss thy shrill monotony of mirth,
And do not love the bars' ferruginous gloss,
When summer nights are blinking-dark and cold,
And the dim taper cheerless to behold.

I thought thee sleeping in some cranny snug,
Insensible to human weal or woe,
Till earlier night bids shake the lazy rug,
And lifts the poker for decisive blow.
But thou hast left thy ashy winter mansion
To air thy crisp-cased wings in wide expansion.

If I should see thee in thy summer dress
'Tis odds if I should know thee, winter friend!
The love I have not, but revere no less,
That can so closely to thy ways attend.
And glad am I the cricket has a share
Of the wide summer, and the ample air.

HARTLEY COLERIDGE [1796–1849]

ON A FLY DRINKING OUT OF HIS CUP

Busy, curious, thirsty fly!
Drink with me and drink as I:
Freely welcome to my cup,
Couldst thou sip and sip it up:
Make the most of life you may,
Life is short and wears away.

Both alike are mine and thine
Hastening quick to their decline:
Thine's a summer, mine's no more,
Though repeated to threescore.
Threescore summers, when they're gone,
Will appear as short as one!

WILLIAM OLDYS [1696–1761]

SPIDER

A spider sewed at night
Without a light
Upon an arc of white.
If ruff it was of dame
Or shroud of gnome,
Himself, himself inform.
Of immortality
His strategy
Was physiognomy.

EMILY DICKINSON [1830–1886]

THE FLEA

Marke but this flea, and marke in this,
How little that which thou deny'st me is;
It suck'd me first, and now sucks thee,
And in this flea, our two bloods mingled bee;
Thou know'st that this cannot be said
A sinne, nor shame, nor losse of maidenhead,
  Yet this enjoys before it wooe,
    And pamper'd swells with one blood made of two,
    And this, alas, is more then we would doe.

Oh stay, three lives in one flea spare,
Where wee almost, yea more than maryed are,
This flea is you and I, and this
Our mariage bed, and mariage temple is;
Though parents grudge, and you, w'are met,
And cloysterd in these living walls of Jet.
    Though use make you apt to kill mee,
      Let not to that, selfe murder added bee,
      And sacrilege, three sinnes in killing three.

  Cruell and sodaine, hast thou since
  Purpled thy naile, in blood of innocence?
  Wherein could this flea guilty bee,
  Except in that drop which it suckt from thee?
  Yet thou triumph'st, and saist that thou
  Find'st not thy selfe, nor mee the weaker now;
    'Tis true, then learne how false, feares bee;
      Just so much honor, when thou yeeld'st to mee,
      Will wast, as this flea's death tooke life from thee.

JOHN DONNE [1572–1631]

THE MURMUR OF A BEE

The murmur of a bee
A witchcraft yieldeth me.
If any ask me why,
'Twere easier to die
Than tell.

The red upon the hill
Taketh away my will;
If anybody sneer,
Take care, for God is here,
That's all.

The breaking of the day
Addeth to my degree;
If any ask me how,
Artist, who drew me so,
Must tell!

EMILY DICKINSON [1830–1886]

BUTTERFLY

From cocoon forth a butterfly
As lady from her door
Emerged – a summer afternoon –
Repairing everywhere,

Without design, that I could trace,
Except to stray abroad
On miscellaneous enterprise
The clovers understood.

Her pretty parasol was seen
Contracting in a field
Where men made hay, then struggling hard
With an opposing cloud,

Where parties, phantom as herself,
To Nowhere seemed to go
In purposeless circumference,
As 'twere a tropic show.

And notwithstanding bee that worked,
And flower that zealous blew,
This audience of idleness
Disdained them, from the sky,

Till sundown crept, a steady tide,
And men that made the hay,
And afternoon, and butterfly,
Extinguished in its sea.

EMILY DICKINSON [1830–1886]

FIREFLIES

Softly sailing emerald lights
  Above the cornfields come and go,
  Listlessly wandering to and fro:
The magic of these July nights
  Has surely even pierced down deep
  Where the earth's jewels unharmed sleep,

And filled with fire the emeralds there
And raised them thus to the outer air.

WILLIAM SHARP [1855–1905]

THE GRASSHOPPER

Voice of the summer-wind,
Joy of the summer-plain,
Life of the summer-hours,
Carol clearly, bound along.
No Tithon thou as poets feign
(Shame fall 'em they are deaf and blind)
But an insect lithe and strong,
Bowing the seeded summer-flowers.
Prove their falsehood and thy quarrel,
Vaulting on thine airy feet.
Clap thy shielded sides and carol,
    Carol clearly, chirrup sweet.
Thou art a mailéd warrior in youth and strength complete;
    Armed cap-a-pie,
    Full fair to see;
    Unknowing fear,
    Undreading loss,
A gallant cavalier,
Sans peur et sans reproche,
In sunlight and in shadow,
The Bayard of the meadow.

I would dwell with thee,
   Merry grasshopper,
Thou art so glad and free,
   And as light as air;
Thou hast no sorrow or tears,
Thou hast no compt of years.
No withered immortality,

But a short youth sunny and free.
Carol clearly, bound along,
   Soon thy joy is over,
A summer of loud song,
   And slumbers in the clover.
   What has thou to do with evil
In thine hour of love and revel,
In thy heat of summer-pride,
   Pushing the thick roots aside
   Of the singing flowerèd grasses,
   That brush thee with their silken tresses?
   What hast thou to do with evil,
   Shooting, singing, ever springing
   In and out the emerald glooms,
Ever leaping, ever singing,
   Lighting on the golden blooms?

LORD TENNYSON [1809–1892]

WILD BEES

These children of the sun which summer brings
As pastoral minstrels in her merry train
Pipe rustic ballads upon busy wings
And glad the cotters' quiet toils again.
The white-nosed bee that bores its little hole
In mortared walls and pipes its symphonies,
And never absent couzen, black as coal,
That Indian-like bepaints its little thighs,
With white and red bedight for holidays,
Right earlily a-morn do pipe and play
And with their legs stroke slumber from their eyes.
And aye so fond they of their singing seem
That in their holes abed at close of day
They still keep piping in their honey dreams,
And larger ones that thrum on ruder pipe
Round the sweet smelling closen and rich woods
Where tawny white and red flush clover buds
Shine bonnily and bean fields blossom ripe,
Shed dainty perfumes and give honey food
To these sweet poets of the summer fields;
Me much delighting as I stroll along
The narrow path that hay laid meadow yields,
Catching the windings of their wandering song.
The black and yellow bumble first on wing
To buzz among the sallow's early flowers,
Hiding its nest in holes from fickle spring
Who stints his rambles with her frequent showers;
And one that may for wiser piper pass,
In livery dress half sables and half red,
Who laps a moss ball in the meadow grass
And hoards her stores when April showers have fled;

And russet commoner who knows the face
Of every blossom that the meadow brings,
Starting the traveller to a quicker pace
By threatening round his head in many rings:
These sweeten summer in their happy glee
By giving for her honey melody.

JOHN CLARE [1793–1864]

MIDGE

Whence do ye come, ye creatures? Each of you
Is perfect as an angel! wings and eyes
Stupendous in their beauty – gorgeous dyes
In feathery fields of purple and of blue!
Would God I saw a moment as ye do!
I would become a molecule in size,
Rest with you, hum with you, or slanting rise
Along your one dear sunbeam, could I view
The pearly secret which each tiny fly –
Each tiny fly that hums and bobs and stirs,
Hides in its little breast eternally
From you, ye prickly, grim philosophers
With all your theories that sound so high:
Hark to the buzz a moment, my good sirs!

GEORGE MACDONALD [1824–1905]

THE GRASSHOPPER

Happy *Insect*, what can be
In happiness compar'd to Thee?
Fed with nourishment divine,
The dewy *Mornings* gentle *Wine*!
Nature waits upon thee still,
And thy verdant Cup does fill,
'Tis fill'd where ever thou dost tread,
Nature selfe's *thy Ganimed*.
Thou dost drink, and dance, and sing;
Happier then the happiest *King*!
All the *Fields* which thou dost see,
All the *Plants* belong to *Thee*,
All that *Summer Hours* produce,
Fertile made with early juice.
Man for thee does sow and plow;
Farmer He, and *Land-Lord Thou*!
Thou doest innocently joy;
Nor does thy *Luxury* destroy;
The *Shepherd* gladly heareth thee,
More *Harmonious* then *He*.
Thee Country Hindes with gladness hear,
Prophet of the ripened year!
Thee *Phoebus* loves, and does inspire;
Phoebus is himself thy *Sire*.
To thee of all things upon earth,
Life is no longer then thy *Mirth*.
Happy *Insect*, happy Thou,
Dost neither *Age*, nor *Winter* know.
But when thou'st drunk, and danc'd, and sung,
Thy fill, the flowry Leaves among
(*Voluptuous*, and *Wise* with all,
Epicuræan Animal!)
Sated with thy *Summer Feast*,
Thou retir'est to endless *Rest*.

ABRAHAM COWLEY [1618–1667]

THE FLIES

    Say, sire of insects, mighty Sol,
(A Fly upon the chariot pole
Cries out,) what Blue-bottle alive
Did ever with such fury drive?
Tell Belzebub, great father, tell,
(Says t'other, perch'd upon the wheel,)
Did ever any mortal Fly
Raise such a cloud of dust as I?
    My judgment turn'd the whole debate:
My valour sav'd the sinking state.
So talk two idle buzzing things;
Toss up their heads, and stretch their wings.
But let the truth to light be brought:
This neither spoke, nor t'other fought:
No merit in their own behaviour:
Both rais'd, but by their party's favour.

MATTHEW PRIOR [1664–1721]

GRASSHOPPERS

Grasshoppers go in many a thrumming spring
And now to stalks of tasseled sow-grass cling,
That shakes and swees awhile, but still keeps straight;
While arching oxeye doubles with his weight.
Next on the cat-tail-grass with farther bound
He springs, that bends until they touch the ground.

JOHN CLARE [1793–1864]

WASP IN A ROOM

Chase me, follow me round the room, knock over
Chairs and tables, bruise knees, spill books. High
I am then. If you climb up to me I go
Down. I have ways of detecting your least
Movements. I have radar you did not
Invent. You are afraid of me. I can
Sting hard. Ah but watch me bask in
The, to you, unbearable sun. I sport with it, am
Its jester and also its herald. Fetch a
Fly whisk. I scorn such. You must invent stings
For yourselves or else leave me alone, small, flying,
Buzzing tiger who have made a jungle out of the room
      you thought safe,
Secure from all hurts and prying.

ELIZABETH JENNINGS [1926–   ]

MYTHICAL
CREATURES

UNNATURAL CREATURES

from: Anti-Jacobin

First – to each living thing, whate'er its kind,
Some lot, some part, some station is assign'd.
The feather'd race with pinions skim the air –
Not so the mackerel, and still less the bear:
This roams the wood, carnivorous, for his prey!
That with soft roe pursues his watery way:
This slain by hunters, yields his shaggy hide;
That, caught by fishers, is on Sundays cried. –

But each, contented with his humble sphere,
Moves unambitious through the circling year;
Nor e'er forgets the fortunes of his race,
Nor pines to quit, or strives to change, his place.
Ah! who has seen the mailed lobster rise,
Clap his broad wings, and soaring claim the skies?
When did the owl, descending from her bower,
Crop, midst the fleecy flocks, the tender flower?
Or the young heifer plunge, with pliant limb,
In the salt wave, and fish-like strive to swim?

JOHN HOOKHAM FRERE [1769–1846]

THE CONSTANT PHOENIX

from: The Phoenix and the Turtle

Here the anthem doth commence:
Love and constancy is dead;
Phoenix and the turtle fled
In a mutual flame from hence.

So they loved, as love in twain
Had the essence but in one;
Two distincts, division none:
Number there in love was slain.

Hearts remote, yet not asunder;
Distance, and no space was seen
'Twixt the turtle and his queen:
But in them it were a wonder.

So between them love did shine,
That the turtle saw his right
Flaming in the phoenix' sight:
Either was the other's mine.

WILLIAM SHAKESPEARE [1564–1616]

THE DRAGON

from: The Faerie Queen (Canto XI)

By this, the dreadful beast drew nigh to hand,
Halfe flying and halfe footing in his haste,
That with his largenesse measured much land,
And made wide shadow under his huge waste;
As mountaine doth the valley overcaste.
Approching nigh, he reared high afore
His body monstrous, horrible, and vaste;
Which, to increase his wondrous greatnes more,
Was swoln with wrath and poyson, and with bloody gore;

And over all with brazen scales was armd,
Like plated cote of steele, so couched neare
That nought mote perce; ne might his corse be harmd
With dint of swerd, nor push of pointed speare:
Which, as an eagle, seeing pray appeare,
His aery plumes doth rouze full rudely dight;
So shaked he, that horror was to heare:
For, as the clashing of an armor bright,
Such noyse his rouzed scales did send unto the knight.

His flaggy winges, when forth he did display,
Were like two sayles, in which the hollow wynd
Is gathered full, and worketh speedy way: ·
And eke the pennes, that did his pineons bynd,
Were like mayne-yardes with flying canvas lynd;
With which whenas him list the ayre to beat,
And there by force unwonted passage fynd,
The cloudes before him fledd for terror great,
And all the hevens stood still amazed with his threat.

His huge long tayle, wownd up in hundred foldes,
Does overspred his long bras-scaly back,
Whose wreathed boughtes when even he unfoldes,
And thick-entangled knots adown does slack,
Bespotted as with shieldes of red and blacke,
It sweepeth all the land behind him farre,

And of three furlongs does but litle lacke;
And at the point two stinges infixed arre,
Both deadly sharp, that sharpest steele exceeden farre.

But stinges and sharpest steele did far exceed
The sharpnesse of his cruell rending clawes:
Dead was it sure, as sure as death indeed,
What ever thing does touch his ravenous pawes,
Or what within his reach he ever drawes.
But his most hideous head my tongue to tell
Does tremble; for his deepe devouring iawes
Wyde gaped, like the griesly mouth of hell,
Through which into his darke abysse all ravin fell.

And, that more wondrous was, in either iaw
Threeranckes of yron teeth enraunged were,
In which yett trickling blood, and gobbets raw,
Of late devoured bodies did appeare;
That sight thereof bredd cold congealed feare:
Which to increase, and all at once to kill,
A cloud of smoothering smoke, and sulphure seare,
Out of his stinking gorge forth steemed still,
That all the ayre about with smoke and stench did fill.

EDMUND SPENSER [1552–1599]

239

THE KRAKEN

Below the thunders of the upper deep;
Far, far beneath in the abysmal sea,
His ancient, dreamless, uninvaded sleep
The Kraken sleepeth: faintest sunlights flee
About his shadowy sides: above him swell
Huge sponges of millennial growth and height;
And far away into the sickly light,
From many a wondrous grot and secret cell
Unnumber'd and enormous polypi
Winnow with giant arms the slumbering green.
There hath he lain for ages and will lie
Battening upon huge seaworms in his sleep,
Until the latter fire shall heat the deep;
Then once by man and angels to be seen,
In roaring he shall rise and on the surface die.

LORD TENNYSON [1809–1892]

PHOENIX

from: The Vision of Petrarch

I saw a Phœnix in the wood alone,
With purple wings, and crest of golden hewe;
Strange bird he was, whereby I thought anone,
That of some heavenly wight I had the vewe;
Untill he came unto the broken tree,
And to the spring, that late devoured was.
What say I more? each thing at last we see
Doth passe away: the Phœnix there alas,
Spying the tree destroid, the water dride,
Himselfe smote with his beake, as in disdaine,
And so foorthwith in great despight he dide,
That yet my heart burnes in exceeding paine,
  For ruth and pitie of so haples plight:
  O let mine eyes no more see such a sight!

EDMUND SPENSER [1552–1599]

THE UNICORN FIGHTS THE LION

from: The Faerie Queen (Book II)

Like as the lyon, whose imperial powre
A proud rebellious unicorn defyes,
T' avoide the rash assault and wrathfull stowre
Of his fiers foe, him to a tree applyes,
And when him ronning in full course he spyes,
He slips aside; the whiles that furious beast
His previous horne, sought of his enimyes,
Strikes in the stroke, ne thence can be released,
But to the victor yields a bounteous feast.

EDMUND SPENSER [1552–1599]

THE GRIFFIN

from: La Semaine

The Indian griffin with the glistring eyes,
Beak eagle-like, back sable, sanguin brest,
White (swan-like) wings, fierce talons alwaies prest
For bloody battails; for, with these he tears
Boars, lions, horses, tigress, bulls and bears:
With these our grandams fruitful panch he puls,
Whence many an ingot of pure gold he culls,
To floor his proud nest, builded strong and steep
On a high rock, better his thefts to keep.

GUILLAUME SALLUSTE DU BARTAS [1544–1590]
(*Translated by* JOSHUA SYLVESTER, 1605)

THE CENTAURS

('THE UNITED IDOLATERS')

Up came the young Centaur-colts from the plains they
    were fathered in –
Curious, awkward, afraid.
Burrs on their hocks and their tails, they were branded and
    gathered in
Mobs and run up to the yard to be made.

Starting and shying at straws, with sidlings and plungings,
    Buckings and whirlings and bolts;
Greener than grass, but full-ripe for their bridlings and
    lungings,
    Up to the yards and to Chiron they bustled the colts . . .

First the light web and the cavesson; then the linked keys
    To jingle and turn on the tongue. Then, with cocked
        ears,
The hours of watching and envy, while comrades at ease
    Passaged and backed, making naught of these terrible
        gears.

Next, over-pride and its price at the low-seeming fence,
    Too oft and too easily taken – the world-beheld fall!
And none in the yard except Chiron to doubt the immense,
    Irretrievable shame of it all! . . .

Last, the trained squadron, full-charge – the sound of a
        going
    Through dust and spun clods, and strong kicks, pelted
        in as they went,
And repaid at top-speed; till the order to halt without
        slowing
    Showed every colt on his haunches – and Chiron content!

RUDYARD KIPLING [1865–1936]

ODE TO THE CAMELEOPARD

Welcome to Freedom's birth-place – and a den!
 Great Anti-climax, hail!
So very lofty in thy front – but then,
 So dwindling at the tail! –
In truth, thou hast the most unequal legs:
Has one pair gallop'd, whilst the other trotted,
Along with other brethren, leopard-spotted,
O'er Afric sand, where ostriches lay eggs?
Sure thou wert caught in some hard uphill chase,
Those hinder heels still keeping thee in check!
 And yet thou seem'st prepar'd in any case,
 Tho' they had lost the race,
  To win it – by a neck!

That lengthy neck – how like a crane's it looks!
Art thou the overseer of all the brutes?
Or dost thou browze on tip-top leaves or fruits –
Or go a-bird-nesting amongst the roks?
How kindly nature caters for all wants;
Thus giving unto thee a neck that stretches,
 And high food fetches –
To some a long nose, like the elephant's!

Oh! had'st thou any organ to thy bellows,
To turn thy breath to speech in human style,
 What secrets thou might'st tell us,
Where now our scientific guesses fail;
 For instance, of the Nile,
Whether those Seven Mouths have any tail –
 Mayhap thy luck too,
From that high head, as from a lofty hill,
Has let thee see the marvellous Timbuctoo –
Or drink of Niger at its infant rill;
What were the travels of our Major Denham,
 Or Clapperton, to thine
 In that same line,
If thou coulds't only squat thee down and pen 'em!

Strange sights, indeed, thou must have overlook'd,
With eyes held ever in such vantage-stations!
Hast seen, perchance, unhappy white folks cook'd,
And then made free of negro corporations?
Poor wretches saved from cast away three deckers –
        By sooty wreckers –
From hungry waves to have a loss still drearier,
To far exceed the utmost aim of Park –
And find themselves, alas! beyond the mark,
In the *insides* of Africa's Interior!

Live on, Giraffe! genteelest of raff kind! –
Admir'd by noble and by royal tongues! –
        May no pernicious wind,
Or English fog, blight thy exotic lungs!
Live on in happy peace, altho' a rarity,
Nor envy thy poor cousin's more outrageous
        Parisian popularity; –
Whose very leopard-rash is grown contagious,
And worn on gloves and ribbons all about,
        Alas! they'll wear him out! –
So thou shalt take thy sweet diurnal feeds –
When he is stuff'd with undigested straw,
Sad food that never visited his jaw!
And staring round him with a brace of beads!

THOMAS HOOD [1799–1845]

JABBERWOCKY

'Twas brillig, and the slithy toves
   Did gyre and gimble in the wabe;
All mimsy where the borogoves,
    And the mome raths outgrabe.

'Beware the Jabberwock, my son!
   The jaws that bite, the claws that catch!
Beware the Jubjub bird, and shun
    The frumious Bandersnatch!'

He took his vorpal sword in hand:
   Long time the manxome foe he sought –
So rested he by the Tumtum tree,
    And stood awhile in thought.

And as in uffish thought he stood,
   The Jabberwock, with eyes of flame,
Came whiffling through the tulgey wood,
    And burbled as it came!

One, two! One, two! And through and through
   The vorpal blade went snicker-snack!
He left it dead, and with its head
    He went galumphing back.

'And hast thou slain the Jabberwock?
   Come to my arms, my beamish boy!
O frabjous day!   Callooh!   Callay!'
    He chortled in his joy.

'Twas brillig, and the slithy toves
   Did gyre and gimble in the wabe;
All mimsy were the borogoves,
    And the mome raths outgrabe.

LEWIS CARROLL [1832–1898]

THE POBBLE WHO HAS NO TOES

The Pobble who has no toes
  Had once as many as we;
When they said, 'Some day you may lose them all;' –
  He replied, – 'Fish fiddle de-dee!'
And his Aunt Jobiska made him drink,
Lavender water tinged with pink,
For she said, 'The World in general knows
There's nothing so good for a Pobble's toes!'

The Pobble who has no toes,
  Swam across the Bristol Channel;
But before he set out he wrapped his nose,
  In a piece of scarlet flannel.
For his Aunt Jobiska said, 'No harm
'Can come to his toes if his nose is warm;
'And it's perfectly known that a Pobble's toes
'Are safe, – provided he minds his nose.'

The Pobble swam fast and well,
  And when boats or ships came near him
He tinkledy-binkledy-winkled a bell,
  So that all the world could hear him.
And all the Sailors and Admirals cried,
When they saw him nearing the further side, –
'He has gone to fish, for his Aunt Jobiska's
'Runcible Cat with crimson whiskers!'

But before he touched the shore,
    The shore of the Bristol Channel,
A sea-green Porpoise carried away
    His wrapper of scarlet flannel.
And when he came to observe his feet,
Formerly garnished with toes so neat,
His face at once became forlorn
On perceiving that all his toes were gone!

And nobody ever knew
    From that dark day to the present,
Whoso had taken the Pobble's toes,
    In a manner so far from pleasant.
Whether the shrimps or crawfish gray,
Or crafty Mermaids stole them away –
Nobody knew; and nobody knows
How the Pobble was robbed of his twice five toes!

The Pobble who has no toes
    Was placed in a friendly Bark,
And they rowed him back, and carried him up,
    To his Aunt Jobiska's Park.
And she made him a feast at his earnest wish
Of eggs and buttercups fried with fish; –
And she said, – 'It's a fact the whole world knows,
'That Pobbles are happier without their toes.'

EDWARD LEAR [1812–1888]

247

THE MOCK TURTLE'S SONG

'Will you walk a little faster?' said a whiting to a snail.
'There's a porpoise close behind us, and he's treading
    on my tail.
See how eagerly the lobsters and the turtles all advance!
They are waiting on the shingle – will you come and
    join the dance?
Will you, won't you, will you, won't you,
      will you join the dance?
Will you, won't you, will you, won't you,
      won't you join the dance?

'You can really have no notion how delightful it will be,
When they take us up and throw us, with the lobsters,
    out to sea!'
But the snail replied 'Too far, too far!' and gave a look
    askance –
Said he thanked the whiting kindly, but he would not
    join the dance.
Would not, could not, would not, could not,
      would not join the dance.
Would not, could not, would not, could not,
      could not join the dance.

'What matters it how far we go?' his scaly friend replied.
'There is another shore, you know, upon the other side.
The further off from England the nearer is to France –
Then turn not pale, beloved snail, but come and join
    the dance.

Will you, won't you, will you, won't you,
      will you join the dance?
Will you, won't you, will you, won't you,
      won't you join the dance?'

LEWIS CARROLL [1832–1898]

THE QUANGLE WANGLE'S HAT

On the top of the Crumpetty Tree
   The Quangle Wangle sat,
But his face you could not see,
   On account of his Beaver Hat.
For his Hat was a hundred and two feet wide,
With ribbons and bibbons on every side
And bells, and buttons, and loops, and lace,
So that nobody ever could see the face
      Of the Quangle Wangle Quee.

The Quangle Wangle said
   To himself on the Crumpetty Tree, –
'Jam; and jelly; and bread;
   'Are the best of food for me!
'But the longer I live on this Crumpetty Tree,
'The plainer than ever it seems to me
'That very few people come this way,
'And that life on the whole is far from gay!'
      Said the Quangle Wangle Quee.

But there came to the Crumpetty Tree,
   Mr. and Mrs. Canary;
And they said, – 'Did ever you see
   'Any spot so charmingly airy?
'May we build a nest on your lovely Hat?
'Mr. Quangle Wangle, grant us that!
'O please let us come and build a nest
'Of whatever material suits you best,
      'Mr. Quangle Wangle Quee!'

And besides, to the Crumpetty Tree
   Came the Stork, the Duck, and the Owl;
The Snail and the Bumble-Bee,
   The Frog, and the Fimble Fowl;
(The Fimble Fowl, with a Corkscrew leg);
And all of them said, – 'We humbly beg,
'We may build our homes on your lovely Hat, –
'Mr. Quangle Wangle, grant us that!
      'Mr. Quangle Wangle Quee.'

And the Golden Grouse came there,
   And the Pobble who has no toes, –
And the small Olympian bear, –
   And the Dong with a luminous nose.
And the Blue Baboon, who played the flute, –
And the Orient Calf from the Land of Tute, –
And the Attery Squash, and the Bisky Bat, –
All came and built on the lovely Hat
      Of the Quangle Wangle Quee.

And the Quangle Wangle said
   To himself on the Crumpetty Tree, –
'When all these creatures move
'What a wonderful noise there'll be!'
And at night by the light of the Mulberry moon
They danced to the Flute of the Blue Baboon,
On the broad green leaves of the Crumpetty Tree,
And all were as happy as happy could be,
      With the Quangle Wangle Quee.

EDWARD LEAR [1812–1888]

SNARK OR BOOJUM?

from: The Hunting of the Snark

'It's a Snark!' was the sound that first came to their ears,
   And seemed almost too good to be true.
Then followed a torrent of laughter and cheers:
   Then the ominous words 'It's a Boo –'

Then silence. Some fancied they heard in the air
   A weary and wandering sigh
That sounded like '– jum!' but the others declare
   It was only a breeze that went by.

They hunted till darkness came on, but they found
   Not a button, or feather, or mark,
By which they could tell that they stood on the ground
   Where the Baker had met with the Snark.

In the midst of the word he was trying to say,
   In the midst of his laughter and glee,
He had softly and silently vanished away –
   For the Snark was a Boojum, you see.

LEWIS CARROLL [1832–1898]

THE BEASTS OF THE GARDEN OF EDEN

from: Paradise Lost (Book IV)

                   About them frisking playd
All beasts of th' Earth, since wilde, and of all chase
In Wood or Wilderness, Forrest or Den;
Sporting the Lion rampd, and in his paw
Dandl'd the Kid; Bears, Tygers, Ounces, Pards,
Gambold before them, th' unwieldy Elephant
To make them mirth us'd all his might, and wreathd
His Lithe Proboscis; close the Serpent sly
Insinuating, wove with Gordian twine
His breaded train, and of his fatal guile
Gave proof unheeded; others on the grass
Coucht, and now fild with pasture gazing sat,
Or Bedward ruminating; for the Sun
Declin'd was hasting now with prone carreer
To th' Ocean Iles, and in th' ascending Scale
Of Heav'n the Starrs that usher Evening rose.

JOHN MILTON [1608–1674]

252

INDEX
of
POETS

INDEX
of
ANIMALS